WHAT PEOPLE SAY ABOUT
HORSES DON'T TEXT
By Dr. Lew Sterrett

"Dr. Lew has had the single most impact on who I am as a leader and as a human being. As a successful executive his teachings helped me influence others in a positive way in all arenas of life!"

– Lisa Bahash, Principal at Architect Equity, LLC

"These principles will, acted upon, positively change your personal life and your endeavors in life. I highly recommend it."

– Rev. Dale E. Linebaugh, Ph.D

"Even in a 100- year-old successful family business, we find this content to be an essential reminder of what must be applied to assure the next 100 years!"

–Seth DeHart, Co-Owner/General Manager of DeHart Air Conditioning

Horses Don't Text!

By Dr. Lew Sterrett

MISSIONAL PRESS
—NASHVILLE, TN—

ISBN: 978-1-7362821-0-6

Missional Press
Nashville, TN
missionalpressbooks.com

Horses Don't Text!

A barnful of hoof-stompin' tips on
how to improve communication at work!

By Dr. Lew Sterrett

INTRODUCTION

My friend Ryan thought he was doing a great job.

He's the president of a family company, which was started by his grandfather and is one of the largest employers in its community. He worked with good people. The company was profitable and its prospects for the future looked bright.

Then he was invited to meet with the heads of several local companies for some training. The group listened to several lectures about leadership and had a frank discussion about the challenges they faced at work. As the discussion went on, Ryan grew concerned.

While most things were going well at his company, he'd started to worry about how people treated each other, especially during difficult moments. He realized most of the interactions he had with employees revolved around criticism.

The same was true for how people in the company treated one another. Nothing was mean-spirited or disrespectful. It's just that when they had something to say about their work or each other, it was mostly negative and nit-picking. There was very little encouragement or recognition when people had done a good job.

People in the company had fallen into some bad habits. Most of those habits, he realized, they had learned from him. "I was not really happy with what I discovered," he said.

At that point, Ryan could have said, "Oh well," and moved on. None of the habits he discovered were major problems. Besides, he was a good boss at a good company and things were looking up. Why mess with a good thing?

But Ryan isn't the kind of person to overlook a problem—even a small one—when he sees it. He didn't like the way he had been treating people. So, he sought out a leadership coach to talk about his concerns and find a way to address them. That's how we met.

After a few long conversations, Ryan and I identified the problem the company was facing and began thinking about small ways he could get better. We focused on being more encouraging in his words and his example—to point out the positives and acknowledge people when they did well. If he did that, people would start to follow his example.

Rather than telling people they needed to become more positive, Ryan showed them the kind of culture he wanted to build.

He began by practicing at home. Ryan had young children and like many parents, he sometimes got irritated with the day-to-day task of teaching them to do the right things. But in his interactions with his kids, Ryan changed his approach. He kept an eye out for all the times they did something right and praised them.

He also started journaling, writing down things that went well and things that didn't. He wanted to identify two or three techniques that worked with his kids. Then he put those habits into practice at work.

I told Ryan that he'd know he was on the right track when someone complimented him on how positive he'd become. That would be a sign that what had once been a weakness had become a strength.

I thought it might take three months. I was off—by a month.

About four months in, Ryan had a long meeting with one of the key managers in the company. They'd known each other for years and things had been tense between them in the past, especially when problems came up at work.

The meeting went off without a hitch. Then, as the manager was leaving, she stopped at the door.

"I don't know what it is," she told him. "But you've been way more encouraging lately. I appreciate it."

It was a small moment—just a quick word of thanks—but it meant the world to Ryan. That moment was start of a new era for his company. Ryan's small acts of encouragement started a feedback loop. As people saw that their boss valued them and noticed their work, they felt appreciated, which made them want to do better each day. Employees had new motivation and a sense their work mattered.

Ryan and his people began to pursue excellence and to value the small steps needed to improve the company.

"I've started to embrace the concept of getting one percent better today," he says. "You get one percent better today and one percent better tomorrow, and after 100 days, you are 100 percent better."

For nearly four decades, I have worked with hundreds of people like Ryan—company leaders, teachers, managers, pastors, parents—all of them looking for that kind of improvement in their work and their lives.

All did good work. But doing good work was not enough. They wanted something more.

They wanted excellence. And not just excellence in their job performance metrics. They wanted excellence in their relationships. They wanted things to be better than they were. They just didn't quite know how to get there.

That's where I have been able to help, by drawing on the knowledge I've gained in four decades of studying human relationships and from what I've learned in more than 40 years as a horse trainer.

Human beings and horses have a lot more in common than you might think.

Horses are intelligent and strong-willed. They have a desire for strong and healthy relationships. They want to be appreciated. They want to know their place in the world and to be happy in their work. And, they can do great or terrible things—depending on their experience and how they react to the challenges in their lives.

People are the same way. We want strong and healthy relationship. We want to know our place in the world. We want to know that our work matters and more than that, that we matter. We want to be praised and noticed by those around us. And we can do great and awful things—depending on how we are treated and how we experience the world around us.

We rarely talk about these things. We tell each other we are fine, go about our day-to-day work and try to get by the best that we can. So much is left unsaid.

That's true today more than ever. We live in a 24/7 world, where we are all more connected than ever. Yet there's a pandemic of loneliness, where people are starved for human connection and true relationship. Instead of deep friendship and fellowship, we settle for a few glib text messages and assume that's good enough.

That's the great thing about horses: they can't text. They can't talk to you and tell you everything is fine. They don't have the language to explain their feelings, their past experience or their worries and concerns.

They can, however, show you all those things by their actions, if you are willing to pay attention. If you watch listen and watch. If you show them that you are trustworthy. If you make them feel safe so that they can fulfill their potential. And if you notice and reward them when they do the right thing.

Here's the other great thing about horses. They are experts in teaching lessons about leadership. You cannot force a horse to do something they don't want to do. You can persuade them and try to impose on them, but there are limits.

In order to have a successful and productive relationship with a horse, you need their cooperation and friendship. If you can win a horse's heart, both you and the horse will prosper and have a fruitful and positive relationship.

To do this, you have to master yourself. You have to remain calm. You have to show the horse how to respect the boundaries that keep both you and the horse safe. You have to give the horse your full attention. You can't glance at your phone while you are working with a horse. You can't be listening with one ear while you are focused on something else.

It's the same with people.

To have healthy relationships at work, at home or in any part of our lives, we have to be present. We have to listen to what people say and more importantly to what they are not saying.
We have to watch their actions and understand what those actions mean.

And we have to show people the way to something better. A life of excellence and meaning and purpose, filled with meaningful work and deep relationships. A life where we fulfill all we were meant to be and to do. And a life where we thrive in both our work and our friendships.

When I was working on this project, I came up with the title "Horses Can't Text."

The idea is that you can't mentor people or learn how to lead from afar, with a few short, quick pithy messages. You've got to spend time with people, getting to know them, earning their trust, learning their stories, and sometimes walking with them through the fire.

There's no magic formula that will make you a successful mentor. But there are tried and true techniques that can help you along the way. I'll pass those on with some stories about how I put them into practice.

The main thing is this: put down your phone.

Stop staring that the little piece of glass and light and instead look around at the people around you—at the office or in the factory, in the classroom or the ball field, in the church or in the community.

Be present.

Pay attention.

Notice the people around you. Listen to what they say. Watch what they do. Catch them doing the right thing and praise them for it. Let them know their good work did not go unnoticed. When they do the wrong thing, talk to them about it. Find out why it happened and how they can avoid making the same mistake twice.

Be like my friend Ryan, who started noticing that things weren't quite right and decided to do something about it.

This is not easy work. Anyone who is a leader—a teacher, a coach, a CEO, a mom or dad—knows that. We have to teach people the right things to do. We have to help them want to do the right thing. We have to, as I like to say, capture their "want to."

This book is about how to do that. It's a companion to the Leaders by HEART training, which teaches lessons in leadership from live demonstrations of working with horses.

In the following chapters, you'll learn some of the techniques in that training. We'll talk about how to set respectful boundaries, how to encourage the people we work with, how to resolve conflict, how to build a team, and how to mentor future leaders.

We'll learn how, as the Bible says, to provoke one another to love and good deeds and excellence—both in performance and relations.

Each chapter will also include a recap of the principles of each step in the process, along with questions that will help you apply what you've learned.

I hope you enjoy the ride.

Some Questions to Consider

1) What thoughts came into your mind when you read about Ryan? Did anything about his story ring true?
2) What are the characteristics of a great leader?
3) Who are some of the leaders you emulate? What about them do you admire?
4) Who are leaders that you dislike? What is about them that drives you away?
5) Why do you want to mentor? What lessons do you want to pass on to those who come after you?

Chapter 1

THE TENDERFOOT

Recently I got a letter telling me I was a terrible person.

The writer had been at a recent Leaders by HEART training and was, to put it mildly, unimpressed.

Having spent more than four decades as a public speaker and leadership coach, I've received my share of negative letters. While many people appreciate what I do, not everyone does. Sometimes people criticizing my speaking style, disagree with something I've said or think that my training methods are wrongheaded or misguided. That's par for the course.

This letter writer, however, went above and beyond the call. I wasn't just a bad speaker or mediocre horse trainer in their eyes. They believed I was a terrible person. And, in the writer's opinion, I had no business having anything to do with horses or teaching leadership.

Besides, the writer claimed I was a bad Christian. They were sure that Jesus would agree.

In short, the writer was not a fan of my work.

What had I done to make this writer so mad? The writer believed I had mistreated a horse named Buddy. They wanted to make sure I was never mean to a horse again.

Let me explain.

A few weeks earlier, I spoke at a company in South Carolina. The company cares about its people and wants to build a culture of respect, where everyone is valued. They asked me to help them do that. I'd been meeting with the staff at the company on a regular basis to talk about leadership over several years.

One morning, I gave a presentation to a group of workers, demonstrating how the principles used in training a horse can help people to communicate better with one another. That morning's presentation was mostly about listening—learning how to pay attention and to build trust by your action, not your words.

As I said in the introduction, you can't text a horse or send them an email. You can't call them on the phone and pass on your instructions. You have to spend time with them, meeting face-to-face. You have to show them you care by investing your time in them. You have to show them what you want them to do in person—not in an email or text. And you have to listen to what they are saying with their body language and attitude.

Sometimes this can be uncomfortable, especially if you are working with a horse (or a person) who wants to be left alone.

That particular morning, my friend Charlie and I were working Buddy, a 9-year-old horse who had never been ridden before. Now Buddy was tall and good looking—a white horse with a few spots of black and brown on his hide. For the most part, he seemed to be a mild-mannered, easy-going horse. Just the kind of horse that anyone would want to ride or pet on the nose.

As I gave my introduction, Buddy stood in the middle of the round pen, grazing contentedly Every once in a while, he'd look at the crowd outside the fence, as if he was wondering what all of the fuss was about.

He seemed happy just to be there on a warm sunny day. Then we got started.

As I stood outside the fence, addressing the company's staff, telling them what we would be doing that morning, Charlie stepped into the round pen with Buddy.

Over the course of about 90 minutes or so, we would do some initial training with Buddy. Charlie led Buddy through a series of exercises while I explained to the onlookers what was happening inside the pen. At the end of our time together, if all went well, Buddy would let Charlie put a saddle on his back and ride him.

At all times we treated Buddy with respect. But we ask him to do things he'd never been asked to do before. And that's where things got interesting.

A few ground-rules

The training had three key components.

First, we set up some boundaries to keep both Buddy and Charlie safe and focused on the job at hand. The boundaries gave us them room to maneuver so neither one could be painted in a corner. At the same time, the boundaries kept Buddy and Charlie in close contact.

There was room for Buddy to breath but not enough room for him to run away.

Second, we gave Buddy our full attention. And we asked him to do the same in return. One of our core beliefs in that you can't build a relationship with someone while you are distracted.

Third, we asked Buddy horse to move —usually by waving a flay at him—and rewarded him for making even the smallest bit of progress.

Each step of the process was broken down into small, bite-sized chunks that helped the horse understand what was expected. After each small step, we rewarded Buddy when he did well and pressed him to try again when he didn't give his best effort.

I've done presentations like this all around the country for decade, taking horses that have had no training and who have never been ridden—sometimes even mustangs who have been running free all of their lives —and in less than two hours, have earned enough of their trust that they will let me ride them.

Most of the horses I work with in these sessions are on the younger side. Buddy was older than most and more set in his ways. Still, he was a good horse and was used to being around people. As long as they didn't get too close or ask him to do something he didn't want to do, he was happy to live and left live.

Try to cross that line, however, and Buddy got ornery. The problem for Buddy is that most of his life, he'd been treated mostly with benign neglect.

For years he'd been owned by a "horse hoarder." A woman collected horses and kept them on a few hundred acres she owned. Some she bought, others she had traded for, some she bred. For the most part, she let the horses run free on her land. She fed them and was kind-hearted, but she lacked the time or energy to care for them and develop healthy relationships with them. Besides looking in on Buddy and the other horses once in a while, she let them run free.

As a result, Buddy liked people as long as they kept their distance. If they got too close, he got nervous. He didn't know how to act around them and became easily spooked. He had never been trained to do even simple tasks like walking into a horse trailer for a visit to the vet.

When it became clear Buddy's owner could not manage the horses, her family took over the property and the care of her horses.

Buddy's new owners, Wes and Marsha, were doing their best to take care of Buddy and the other horses. They'd both grown up around horses, and while they weren't trainers, they knew how to take care of them.

But Buddy was a problem. Even after a year, they'd made very little progress. "He doesn't trust anyone," Marsha said.

Because he didn't trust anyone, Buddy would get spooked easily. Even something basic, like checking his feet or walking him into a horse trailer or visiting the vet, turned into a crisis.

Buddy hadn't been mistreated. But he had been neglected and never learned to have a respectful relationship with people. His new owners wanted to care for Buddy and provide him with a long and happy life. But that wasn't going to be possible unless he learned how to trust them.

That fall morning, we set out to change Buddy's life.

As I mentioned earlier, the first step was setting boundaries. We led Buddy in a round pen, an enclosed area where he'd have space to move but couldn't run away. Then we taught him how to listen, not just with his ears but with his eyes and his feet. We made him move by waving a flag and showing him which way we wanted him to go. And we rewarded him when he paid attention.

We also let Buddy choose whether or not to trust us. When he got nervous, Charlie backed off a bit and gave him breathing room. In other words, we gave Buddy respect and attention and we asked Buddy to return that respect and attention.

Things started slow. But eventually, Buddy started following Charlie around the pen because he wanted to be close to this new friend he made. At the end of an hour and a half, this once shy, confused and distrustful horse let Charlie put a saddle on him and ride him around the pen.

Boundaries. Respect. Listening. Trust. These are the building good of any good relationships—whether it's between a horse and a trainer, an employer and a new employee, a coach and their team, or a teacher and classroom full of students.

All relationships start with these basics and a lot of hard work.

In Buddy's case, we had to get after him some. Because of his trust issues, he wanted to ignore Charlie when the training started. When that didn't work, he tried to run away. Charlie waited him out. While he gave Buddy space, he never let Charlie get too far away. Instead, with patience, kindness and persistence, he continued to invite Buddy into a conversation that would lead to a relationship based on trust. At the end of the session, Buddy was a different horse.

His owners were amazed. They had hope now that life could be different for him. There was a sense of calm around Buddy as if an enormous weight had been lifted off his shoulders.

The letter writer, however, had a different impression. They had watched our training session and felt we had mistreated Buddy by being so direct with him.

Buddy was a nice horse, the writer said. Why didn't we just leave well enough alone? Why put him through the hassle of our training session? Couldn't we see that Buddy was shy and confused and just needed some space? Why put him through so much stress?

These are good questions.

Why go through all this effort to get through to Buddy? Why not just leave him alone?

Because his owners cared too much about Buddy to leave him the way he was and to continue the pattern of treating him with benign neglect. They wanted to see him reach his full potential. And they wanted to help undo the damage that years of benign neglect had caused.

I wish everyone at that session had the chance to talk to Wes and Marsha and see how much they cared about Buddy and how much they worried about him. Or had the chance to see what they had gone through to get Buddy to the training.

Earlier that morning, Wes was loading Buddy into his horse trailer—a fairly low key, routine task—when Buddy balked and banged his head against the wall of the trailer. It took a long time to calm him down and Wes had to be careful to add some extra ropes to keep Buddy from harming himself.

If something simple as getting into a trailer—the horse equivalent of sitting down in a car—caused Buddy to panic, what would happen in a real crisis? What would happen if Buddy was sick and needed medical care, had an injury to his hoofs that needed attention or were stuck somewhere and needed to be helped?

If Buddy panicked in that kind of circumstance, he could hurt the people who were trying to help him or he could lose his life. He would be like a drowning person who grasps so desperately to a lifeguard that both of them are at risk of sinking to the bottom.

Buddy's inability to relate to others and trust them made him an unsafe horse—not bad or intentionally dangerous but unsafe all the same. And no one wants to keep an unsafe horse.
It's not good for the horse or its owners.

The older he got, the more trouble Buddy would be. And if he didn't change, the owners might eventually decide that he was too much trouble to keep around.

In the end, a lot of it was up to Buddy. He had a choice to make: did he want to remain isolated and mistrustful, withdrawing from anyone who tried to get near? Or could he take a risk and let someone else get close to him?

He chose the latter. And it changed his life.

When he walked out of the pen, Buddy was a different horse. Calmer, more relaxed, and more trusting. When Wes and Ruth led him to the trailer, he walked in with no trouble because he'd finally learned how to trust someone else.

"I am thrilled to death that he responded the way he did," Wes said afterward. "It gives us a lot more hope that we can take him home and work with him."

Buddy wasn't a bad horse. He was a lost horse, who needed someone to show him the way to a better life.

There are lots of horses out there like Buddy. And lots of people like Buddy—who have never learned to trust someone else or to have healthy, respectful relationships, where they are respected and give respect in return.

All they need is for someone to take the time to show them a better way.

Over the past four decades, I've traveled the country, training thousands of horses like Buddy and showing how the principles used in training horses can be applied to human relationships.

Those principles—setting clear boundaries, learning to listen, building trust slowly, pursuing excellence, developing sound decision-making skills—can be applied by anyone. With a little time, patience and consistency, the principles can change your life and the life of the people you lead.

We call it "Leadership by HEART." The goal is to build close relationships, so people not only want to do the right thing, but they also know how to make the sound decisions needed to do the right thing.

It starts with a few simple first steps.

Set firm boundaries

I can't emphasize this point enough. All mentoring begins with few clear boundaries.

With a horse, this involves working in a clearly defined space—most often in a round pen that's about 60 feet in diameter. The pen is made up of a series of interlocking fence panels set up in a flat grassy area or an area of well-tamped down dirt. The pen helps us create a space that is safe and comfortable, with good footing and enough space to give both the horse and trainer room to maneuver as we work together. I want us to be close but not crowded.

With your employees, students or employees, this mean setting a few ground rules of how you will work together, such as what time people are supposed to arrive, what their specific job duties are, how they are to treat one another and how they care for the office or the workshop.

In the classroom, it may mean setting up assigned seats, giving clear rules about when to talk and when to listen and how students will treat one another. For a team, this can mean rules about practice times, how to treat the equipment you use and the kind of commitment that's needed to be part of the team.

The key is to make sure people know what is expected of them and to ensure they have a safe environment to work and learn in.

When we set up a round pen, I make sure the ground is level and firm, so there's no chance the horse or trainer will trip or stumble. I make sure the fences panels are locked in place and solid and won't fall over if the horse decides to bump them.

In work or class settings, this may mean making sure the environment is clean, free of hazards and quiet enough for people to be able to get their work done.

Once the pen is set up, either I or one of my team members will lead the horse in and let them get used to their new environment. This usually happens an hour or so before the training session gets starts. That way, the horse has a chance to relax and get comfortable. They can graze a bit or walk around, getting used to the sights, sounds and smells around them.

They can also get used to people who will be watching the presentation. Those folks usually filter in a few at a time and the horse can watch them and get used to them as well. Either I or one of my team members will visit with the horse, reassuring them by rubbing their head or just standing by them.

All this prep work helps create a calm, low-stress environment, that's conducive to learning.

My main role in this first phase of the training is to teach. The horse's main job during this time is to listen. I'm not going to ask them to do anything stressful or complicated. Instead, I want them to pay attention. Being in an environment with some clear boundaries and few distractions makes it easier for the horse to do that.

At the same time, the pen gives them limits. That's mostly to keep them safe. I don't want a horse bolting and running away, which could lead to them being injured or them injuring one of the audience members who have come to see a training session.

The pen also allows me to test the horse to see if I can trust him. Usually, I have a few minutes to talk with owners of a horse to get a sense of their personality and the kind of background they have. That information is helpful, but I still want to check out the horse for myself.

I don't want to ask the horse to do something they aren't ready for. And I want to know whether I can trust them and whether they are willing to trust me. That cuts down on the risks that one of us will be hurt during a training session.

These same principles work with people, especially at the beginning of a new relationship. Whether it's a new employee starting first day on the job, a student beginning school, a team's first practice or a couple going out on a first date. Having clear expectations at the beginning helps that relationship get off on the right foot.

When I hire a new person, I give them some ground rules. I tell them what time to show up, explain what they should bring with them, and how I expect them to act while on the job. Then I give them some simple tasks to see how they handle them.

In the early days, I keep a close eye on them to see how they act in this new environment. Can they show up on time? Can they do the tasks I've asked them to do? How do they treat their co-workers? What happens when they make a mistake—do they clean up the mess they've made or try to cover it up and ignore it?

Setting up a low-stress environment with clear boundaries makes it safe for people to make mistakes when they are starting out and learning a new job, skill or role. It gives me a chance to find out if the new person is a good fit for the job before I send them off on their own.

Communicate clearly

Having set the physical boundaries with the horse, I begin to a few simple directions. This means waving a flag and prompting the horse to run in a certain direction.

For the most part, horses communicate by action. Their communication is almost all physical. They do neigh, snort and make a few other sounds, but that's not their main form of communication. Instead, they speak through their movement and body language.

While training a horse, we want to speak in a way they understand. We listen in the same way, paying close attention to the horse's body language. We want to make sure the horse understands what we are trying to say and we understand what the horse is trying to tell us.

In this way, horses are not that much different than people. When we talk to someone else, we communicate clearly in language they can understand. And we often watch that person's body language to gauge whether we've been understood.

We've all been there. You tell someone to do something or trying to communicate some important information and the other person's eyes glaze over. They start looking at the clock or at their phone—anywhere but at you. Or they sit forward, nod their head and look engaged in what you are saying.

In either case, a person's body language will often tell us more than their words. Most of us have said, "uh-uh" or "yes" to someone else by habit, without really hearing what the other person actually said. That's led to many disagreements at work and at home.

When that happens, we have to back up and get everyone to pay attention to make sure we are all on the same page and seeing the same thing. The same thing applies to horses.

By waving a flag at them, we put subtle pressure on the horse, forcing them to pay attention. Then we look for signs that they are paying attention, that they are acknowledging my presence and giving me a sign they are listening.

A horse will do this by moving in response to a flag being waved. They also do it by looking in my direction. As the old song goes, "just one look" is all we need to know that the horse understands what I am trying to say.

Once the horse looks in my direction, I'll back off on the pressure, because I know I have their attention. They get rewarded every time they make even the slightest sign they are paying attention.

I want the horse to know I am trustworthy. More than that, I want them to see that by trusting me and following my lead their life will get better. That's the point of mentoring after all—to help people grow and develop while aspiring to something greater. But that growth takes time.

In that first meeting with Buddy, I could see what he was capable of and how much better his life could be if only he could learn to trust people. I could see all the possibilities that would be laid out before him if he could take a few easy steps of faith and make a few simple, smart choices. In the short time that Charlie and I had with Buddy, we could not show him his entire future. But we could show him how, on this one day, he could decide to live a better life.

It's not a process that can be rushed because it relies on building trust. And trust is earned one step at a time. Every time I meet a new horse—or a new employee or student—I have to start over. They don't know me. They don't know if I will keep my word and look out for their best interests—or if I will take advantage of them.

So, I set up boundaries and safe environment that are conducive to building trust. I speak clearly and demonstrate that I will keep my word. I never hurry. I don't get angry if something goes wrong.

If the horse makes a mistake, I remember they are learning. At the same time, I don't turn my back on a horse until that horse shows me they are capable of making good decisions. Again, that would be dangerous for both of us. I don't want to give a horse more than they can handle. Setting these initial boundaries gives them a solid foundation for the future.

The same is true for people, whether it's a new employee, a football player stepping on the field for the first time, or a child starting out at school. We begin at the same place—setting the boundaries and expectations that will define our relationship.

The people who work for us or those who we supervise have to get the basics right. They have to show up on time. They have to show that they understand the basic tasks of their job and demonstrate that they can complete them consistently. They have to be able to ask questions if they don't understand what's going on. Most importantly, they have to show the ability to make good decisions while performing small, perfunctory duties.

This is when, as a leader, you need to spend time with your people and keep a close eye on them. There's a lot of teaching and a great deal of observing at the beginning stages of any relationship.

You see how they deal with their fellow employees. You see how they treat the equipment and materials they will be using on the job. You see what they do when something goes wrong or when there is a mess that needs to be cleaned up.

A good leader won't send a new employee out on their own until the person has demonstrated their ability to do the job and has the confidence to do that job on their own. Better they learn—and make their mistakes—when you are around to teach them than for them to be working with customers or others outside your organization before they are ready to do so.

We can't expect people to do the big things right and make wise decisions about major projects if they haven't shown they can handle the small things. If we don't set the right boundaries at the beginning, then we set people up for failure.

Failure means more work for the leader and more headaches for everyone. Setting these boundaries means investing a lot of time on the front end. Doing so can save us time and energy and frustration in the long run.

If things go wrong, sometimes even a leader has to be able to go back to the beginning and start over. That was the case for Charlie, who was a horse trainer and an equine dentist before he started to work with me.

For years, he ran a successful but frustrating equine dentistry practice. There were always problems. His staff didn't do things the way he wanted them done. His clients didn't always pay on time. Most of all he didn't like the work.

As a result, Charlie's days were filled with unpleasant experiences. He'd show up, have a perfunctory conversation with his clients, and then get to work on their horses. As soon as he was done, he left. His only reward was a paycheck. And it seemed like he spent half of his time trying to track people down to get their bills paid. Eventually, Charlie had enough and wanted things to change.

He'd been to a number of my presentations and hosted several events for me. He seemed to think what I had to say was helpful, so he asked me to coach him on leadership. As we talked, we identified the problems he was facing and a few small steps he could take to try and make things better.

For starters, he began spending more time with his clients, seeing them as people rather than a paycheck. The more time they spent together, the better he got to know them and their horses. All of a sudden, days were filled with house calls to see friends rather than series of unpleasant appointments.

As he developed relationships with them, he began to ask more of his clients. If they didn't pay, he called them and asked what was going on. If people repeatedly didn't pay their bills, he politely but firmly told them that not paying was harming their relationship.

In short, he reset the terms of their relationship. Rather than getting mad, he addressed problems in a straightforward manner. As a result, his business became a source of joy in his life rather than a constant frustration. The same approach works for any leader.

If an employee or student or volunteer makes a mistake, you don't get mad or ignore the problem. Instead, you take a step back and reset the boundaries and expectations. You go back to basics and begin rebuilding trust. You take a deep breath, clearly explain what went wrong, and start over.

There's a saying I often use when talking about leaders: Never lower your standards; always adjust your expectations.

When people fail, sometimes it's because they were not ready for the task we asked them to perform. We gave them too much rope or too much responsibility. So, we start over. We ask them to do something simpler. Or we break down the task into smaller steps and check in along the way. That enables us to focus on small wins rather than what is going wrong.

When people do well, we reward them. We look for small signs of success and recognize them. People want to know whether or not they will be rewarded if they do what is expected of them. It doesn't have to be major approval. It doesn't have to be a pay raise. But there has to be an acknowledgment of a job well done.

One last thing to keep in mind: the most dangerous horse is a quiet, passive horse. The one that looks like it wouldn't hurt a fly. On the outside, they may look like a nice horse. And they do what they are asked, to a point. But push them a little bit too far and they will explode, catching everyone by surprise.

That horse is dangerous because they have never been honest. And I cannot let someone else ride a horse until they have been tested and shown that they are trustworthy. Being calm and appearing to be nice isn't good enough. Sometimes under that calm appearance is a lot of trouble.

Speak the truth

Let's go back to our friend Buddy.

It took a while for him to learn to pay attention to Charlie during the training presentation. Buddy would take a few steps forward and then he'd lose momentum. At times he'd move away from Charlie or turn his head and refuse to acknowledge him.

It was hard for Buddy to learn to trust Charlie. If he had not been in the round pen Buddy would have bolted and run off somewhere far from Charlie and everyone else. Being in the pen meant that was no longer an option

All the while, Charlie made it easy for Buddy to make a different choice. With his actions, he demonstrated that he cared about Buddy and wanted to have a relationship with him. Charlie consistently told the truth and was reliable. He was calm and in control, never overreacting, no matter what Buddy did. And he rewarded Buddy for doing the right thing. Charlie showed Buddy that he could be trusted—that he would stick with Buddy and not give up on him.

When I do a presentation, I often remind people that every relationship is built on two foundational principles: trust and truth. We tell the truth and we prove are trustworthy. Nobody will trust someone who has proved to be a liar. And no one, in the end, will trust someone who is unpredictable—someone who is angry and not safe to be around.

I've seen trainers and leaders who lie, get angry and become unsafe. Sometimes, they are also successful—at least at first. You can lie to people and get them to follow you, but eventually those lies catch up to you. You can force people to do what you want, but at some point, you'll push too far. At that point, the people who have followed you will either leave or just go through the motions because they have been crushed.

Real leadership involves trust and truth that allows people to grow and develop and feel appreciated. And it starts from the very beginning—with every word you say and every action you take. Charlie demonstrated that with Buddy.

About halfway through the training session, I saw Buddy had started to make some progress. So, I asked Charlie to call Buddy to him. At that time, Buddy and Charlie were about 20 feet apart.

Charlie looked at Buddy and began to call him, by making kissing sounds and looking at him.

Buddy began to move one of his feet and then stopped and turned away. He chewed his lips, a sign that he was trying to make up his mind. He wanted to be near Charlie but was afraid to take that first step.

I had Charlie turn and walk away. Then he stopped and called again. Again Buddy wavered and looked away. Then Charlie called a third time. Buddy chewed his lips and hesitated. Charlie waited and then turned away from Buddy and stared to walk away. This time Buddy started to follow him. The whole crowd, who had been holding their breath with anticipation, let out an audible sigh.

Over the next few minutes, Charlie led Buddy around the pen without a rope and without touching his bridle. Every once in a while, he'd turn and rub Buddy's head and whisper a few words of affirmation. Then they'd walk some more. Before long, Buddy let Charlie put a blanket on him and then a saddle. Finally, he let Charlie climb on his back and the two went for a ride around the pen.

You could see in Buddy's face and his body language that all the tension was gone. He was, perhaps for the first time, enjoying someone else's company. He was at ease and knew exactly what was expected of him. More than that, he was experiencing the simple joy of having made a friend—having an honest and respectful relationship with someone else.

There was still a lot of work to do. One morning's training session wouldn't change Buddy's life forever. But he'd opened the door into a brighter future. As his owners led him away, I could see that he was a different horse and was on his way to a better life.

Looking Back

In this chapter, we talked about basic building blocks of mentoring:

- Set firm boundaries
- Communicate clearly
- Go slow
- Reward forward motion
- Speak the truth

Some Questions to Consider

1) What are some ways you can apply these principles in your workplace?
2) Is there one person—an employee, a student, someone on your team—who could benefit from these principles?
3) Which of these principles would be hardest for you to apply?
4) Have you ever met someone like Buddy? What about the story rang true?
5) Do you have people in your life like Charlie that you can rely on to have your back when a crisis hits?
6) What do you know at the end of this chapter that you did not know at the beginning?

Looking Ahead

The most important thing a mentor can do is capture the "want-to" of the people we lead. In the next chapter, we'll talk about the process of getting people to want to do the right thing and how to help them catch a vision of something greater than themselves.

Chapter 2

BRONCBUSTER

Over the past 50 years, I've worked with thousands of horses. They generally fall into one of three categories.

There are the "want-to" horses, who are eager to get the job done. They don't have to be asked twice and often exceed expectations. They are a joy to be around and throw themselves into the work wholeheartedly.

There are the "have-to" horses. They get the job done if you push them a bit. They're steady and reliable if you keep an eye on them.

Then there are "just try and make me" horses. If they do something, it's always on their terms and usually because there is something in it for them. You can get their cooperation if they feel like it. If they don't— watch out.

Splash was that kind of horse.

We met not long after I'd worked with Buddy. Like Buddy, Splash was an older horse who had reached a dead end.

His owners had bought him thinking he was what's known as a "bomb proof" horse—one so well- trained and calm that he wouldn't panic even if a bomb went off beside him. Sometimes known as a "babysitter," this kind of horse is one you'd buy for child or for a new rider, just starting out. Completely safe and even-tempered and not bothered by having to carry an inexperienced rider, no matter what happens.

Splash certainly looked the part. That morning, he stood in the middle of the round pen, calmly grazing and looking like he didn't have a care in the world. He sidled over to Kami, one of my team members, and let her stroke his neck. Friendly and unassuming, Splash seemed like the most well behaved and likable horse you could ever meet.

Five minutes later he was trying to kick me in the face. All because I'd asked him to do something he did not want to do.

Over the next hour, Splash would go from perfectly calm to out of control. He would race around the pen and at one point bucked so hard he crashed into the fence and knocked himself over and then he would stop and start to graze as if he hadn't a care in the world.

You may know a few people like this. They're perfectly calm and friendly as long as you don't cross them or push them to do something they don't want to do, then they turn on you. Their responses are always over the top. They're like a timebomb, quietly ticking away, waiting to go off.

In the last chapter, we talked about the important of setting boundaries and expectations, creating an environment where everyone is safe and knows what is expected of them. This is an environment where everyone is treated with respect and people are asked to live up to the promises they made.

This chapter is about speaking the truth. That involves getting past the superficial niceties where we pretend everything is fine, we don't talk about how things are really going, and especially avoid things that aren't working.

With Splash I'd set up a safe environment and ground rules. Now I wanted him to tell me truth. I wanted him to drop the façade and be honest. Then we would make some progress. It would have been easier to write him off. There was a lot of risk in working with Splash and little hope of reward. He was like a black hole, ready to suck up all your time and energy and never give anything back.

We all know people who are seemingly not worth the hassle. We either put up with them by spending all our time trying to appease them and keep them on an even keel, or we just write them off. None of those approaches are satisfying. None would work for Splash. It was too late for that. Either he was going to change or he'd be out options.

In the time we had together, Splash had to make up his mind. Did he want to make a change for the better? Or was happy with the way things were?

I hoped Splash would change because if he did, a whole world of new possibilities would open up to him. That's something I know firsthand. You see, in some ways, I used to be like Splash, determined to do what I wanted, willing to run over anyone who got in my way. Then a horse named Nava Rose changed my life.

At the time, I was a young horse trainer and something of a hotshot. I was working for an older trainer and had several prestigious awards. My methods then were pretty blunt. I didn't abuse horses, but I'd keep the pressure on until a horse bent to my will.

And at first, I tried to get them to do what I wanted with a mix of kindness and pressure. If that didn't work, I tried to force them to do what I want. I didn't know then about the importance of building a relationship with a horse or the importance of focusing on long term goals rather than short-term successes. All I wanted from my horses was for them to do what they were told. Nava Rose could not do that.

She was a three-year-old mare with great potential. My boss thought she could someday be a national champion show horse. Because he believed in me, he entrusted Nava Rose to me. As I recounted in my book, *Life Lessons from a Horse Whisperer*, things went well at first. She'd already had some training and knew the basics and was ready to start advanced training.

Things came to a head, however, when I tried to teach a fairly complicated task, involving an old tire. For this maneuver, she had to put her front feet in the tire and then turn in a circle by rotating her back legs. It's a complicated maneuver but not overly difficult.

A horse with Nava Rose's talent should have been able to master it pretty quickly. Except that she couldn't get it. After a few tries, she got nervous and frustrated. Eventually, she started backing up, taking her feet out of the hollow center of the tire.

Had I known her better, or been a better trainer, I would have stopped right there. She wasn't trying to be disobedient or difficult. She was confused, worried and needed my help. She needed to know she could trust me to guide her, not to punish her.

By taking her feet out of the center of the tire, Nava Rose was sending a clear message. *I'm confused*, she was saying. *I need help.* I was not listening.

In that moment, I lost my cool. I grabbed her by the head and yanked her to the ground. I wanted to show her that I was stronger than she was, that she could not disobey me. She got that message loud and clear.

She got up quickly and ran as far away from me as she could. Nava Rose was terrified and knew right then I could not be trusted. Something broke in me that moment.

When I realized what I had done, I was ashamed and began to cry. Slowly but sure, I was able to heal that relationship, but it took a long time. I had to rebuild her confidence and show her that I was trustworthy.

Now most leaders don't shove their workers to the ground. But we are tempted to use our authority to force people to follow us. Or we too easily lose our temper and get people to do what we want by humiliating or demeaning them instead of showing them the respect they deserve.

Remember what we talked about in the last chapter: the first thing a mentor has to do is show they are trustworthy. I didn't understand that when I first worked with Nava Rose. Up to that point, I'd gotten by on natural talent and force of will. I had a knack for working with horses and had been lucky to work with horses who were a good fit for my style.

But I'd never been tested. It's easy to be trustworthy when things are going well. It's much harder when things go wrong. The truth was I was not trustworthy at that moment. I was lucky enough to learn that early on.

In that time with Nava Rose, I decided to become someone different. I spent months proving to her and the other horses I was someone she could trust. And the decisions I made day by day from then on changed my life.

Today, I want the horse to do their best and be happy doing it—not to do their best because they are afraid of me.

Preparing for conflict

A leader needs to self-aware. You have to be in the right state of mind and be in control of yourself. Especially if you are walking into a situation that may involve conflict. Never assume you can coast along on your skills or position.

Instead, you have to prepare your heart ahead of time and set aside any distractions that might keep you from the task at hand. If you can't do that, best to put things off until another day.

I may look calm and collected in the round pen with a horse but on the inside, I am just like everyone else. I get nervous.

When I am about to deal with a situation that is difficult or could lead to conflict, I get a knot in my stomach and sweat on my palms. When that happens, I take a deep breath, let go of my worries, and trust in my planning and preparation.

A leader needs to be filled with grace, especially when they are under pressure. We have to be calm and confident and focused on the task at hand. The book of Proverbs puts it this way: "A gentle answer turns away wrath, but a harsh word stirs up anger."

One way to put this advice into practice is to always be prepared.

Before I start a training session, I think through what might happen and how I will react. I keep my eyes focused on what's in front of me. I leave all the distractions behind when I walk into a round pen with a horse. I can't be worried about what the audience is thinking, paying the bills, the disagreement I had with my wife, or any of the million other things that may cloud my mind.

To help me focus, I begin every session by setting expectations for my audience. I tell them what I am going to do and what might happen. During the training, I never rush or worry about impressing the audience. Instead, I focus on doing my best to help the horse in the arena with me reach its potential.

And I never forget that things won't always go the way I planned. If things don't go well, I take a deep breath and keep at the work in a calm and persistent manner.

In the end, I want the horse to win. I want them to know that by trusting someone else and by giving up on having their own way all the time, their lives will be richer.

I want them to experience a trusting relationship with their trainer and to see how much better their life will be because of that relationship. And I hope the example of the horse and trainer will rub off on the people who are watching.

When I get after a horse, it's not because I hate him, it's because I want him to be a better horse. As a leader, I get after people because I want them to be better people. I don't get after people or a horse to provoke them to anger. I am trying to provoke them to excellence, to help them move from where they are to where they could be.

A look at real life

Let's take this out of the round pen for a minute.

As leaders, much of our job involves putting pressure on people and watching what happens next. We ask our people questions, give them assignments, and see how they respond. Do they respond willingly and put forth good effort? Do they look for ways to delay and get out of the assignment? Can they do the job we've asked them to do?

Along the way, we look for ways to affirm the worth of a person, even if we have to critique their performance. The whole point is to show our people that we care for them, and that we care enough to want them to excel.

Take the case of a worker who consistently misses deadlines. This should concern me as a leader. Missing a deadline can have a ripple effect on the rest of the team and can even affect customers or others outside of my organization.

Before I take any action, I want to sort out exactly what is happening. This involves a series of questions: Is this person missing the deadline because they don't understand the work? Is it because they didn't have time? Have I given them too many tasks to do at the same time?

Do they not understand why hitting the deadline matters? Do they not care about hitting the deadline?

The first few questions are about execution. The last is about attitude.

Sometimes when a worker fails, we see it as a character flaw and get angry at them for messing with our plans. As leaders, we might assume something is wrong with the person and they intentionally let us down.

A better approach is to gather some facts and see exactly what's going on, so we can fix the problem.

We need to make sure our people understand what we are asking them to do and why it matters. We need to make sure they have the skills, the training, and the time to do the job we've asked them to do. And we need to identify the obstacles that stand in the way of getting the job done.

So, we assign tasks, ask questions, and gather information. Then we act.

Two other things to consider: First, you can only speak as loud as the other person can hear. Second, you can only ride one horse at a time.

Sometimes we think that if someone isn't doing what we want, we just need to get louder. We repeat our instructions and raise our voice. Often, as the decibels rise so do the threats. That is a recipe for disaster. Even if the person does what we want, we end up damaging the relationship — as I did when I was a young trainer with Nava Rose.

Most of the time, we get better results by lowering our voices and doing more explaining.

That's one reason, as I said earlier, I make sure I clear my mind and block out distractions when I enter the round pen with a new horse. I've got to be calm and focused on the task at hand, for my own sake and for the sake of the horse.

The work I do is potentially dangerous—a full-grown horse is a powerful animal that can weigh 1,000 pounds or more. If things get out of hand, the horse or I could be hurt. I could even be killed if I am not careful.

Since I am the leader, it's my job to ensure the situation remains safe and stable. I can't afford to overreact, lose my temper, or provoke the horse so that it loses control. That's bad for everyone.

If you've been a leader for any length of time, you know the same can be said for people. Most of us have been in a situation where one wrong word or a misinterpreted action leads to a blow-up or disaster.

Sometimes the best thing to do is take a deep breath and wait a minute before saying something you regret.

When a leader does choose to speak, they have to do so in a way that the other person can hear.

Remember, every relationship is unique.

As I said before, you can only ride one horse at a time. Even if you are a leader of a group, you have to work individually with each person in the group.

Often as leaders, we expect everyone else to adapt to our style of communication and our way of doing things. But a great leader can speak in the language of their followers.

Say you have someone on your team who is quiet and introverted. Putting them on the spot in front of a group won't likely lead to great results. Raising your voice with them will shut them down completely.

What if you have someone on the team who is a people-pleaser? They may say yes to everything you ask them to do and then not be able to deliver because they are overwhelmed. Or they might focus on a short-term task you give them and neglect their long-term projects.

Some team members need you to be blunt with them and don't mind criticism. Others prefer a more indirect approach and might need to be reassured that they are doing well before you can critique them.

There are likely some people on your team who are calm in a crisis and can change directions quickly. Others aren't able to stop on a dime and do something new. They may need to talk things out before they feel comfortable with changes of plan.

Just like you can't make a horse do what you want them to do, you can't make people do what you want them to do. You can try to force them to follow your instructions. That works for a while. But in end, they will either defy you openly or find a million ways to avoid doing what you've asked.

If you can capture their hearts if you can get people to trust you and buy into your leadership—anything is possible.

In his book, *Everybody Matters: The Extraordinary Power of Treating Your People Like Family*, author Bob Chapman, described how the power of trust helped turn his family's company from a dying business to a thriving, billion-dollar company.

As the CEO of Barry-Wehmiller, a major manufacturer, he'd once been driven entirely by profits. Then sitting in a church, watching a friend's daughter get married, he had a bit of a revelation. Chapman said at that moment, he realized that everyone who worked for him was like that young married couple—someone's beloved child. He began to wonder what might happen if his company began to treat people as if they matter.

More than that, he wondered, what might happen if the company gave people a say in how things were run. What if leadership listened to ideas from the workers, rather than dictating how the company was run? Could they treat the people who worked at the company as if they were family and not just hired help?

The company began to change the way it did business, eventually building a culture of trust, relationship, and a commitment to excellence.

"We believe, and have repeatedly experienced, that if you take care of your people, they will take care of the business," he wrote. "If you genuinely let them know that they matter, they will respond in kind. Trust is the foundation of leadership; if you trust people, they will trust you back."

This resonates with almost everything I've learned studying and teaching about leadership. Trust and respect are the foundation of any successful human endeavor—a business, a team, a school or a family. And for four decades, I've tried to teach people how to build respect-filled and trustful relationships with the help of my horses.

Will you trust me?

Every principle I use to train horses can be applied to human relationships, especially when it comes to trust, patience, and respect. Those three things are the basic building blocks of human relationships and team building.

My role in the process is to pay attention to the horse and look out for their well-being. I want to show by my actions that I am trustworthy, and that I will apply everything I've learned over my 40 years of experience towards helping them be successful.

To show the difference that trusting relationships can make, I often pair my horse, Hansom, with an untrained horse. Hansom—a palomino who is half Arabian, half Quarter Horse—and I have worked together for years. We are so in tune that I can ride him without reins or a bridle, guiding him with the slightest bit of pressure from one of my knees.

During our time together, I paired up Splash with Hansom and ran them through a few basic tasks, the kinds of things that are routine for almost every horse.

First, I asked them to let me put a bit in their mouths. Then I asked them to move their back hips towards me. Finally, I asked them to let me put a rope around their bellies—in preparation for saddling them.

All of these were quite ordinary, reasonable requests for a horse. I was looking for a similarly reasonable response to each request.

Things went off without a hitch with Hansom. He handled every request with ease and breezed through each task in a matter of minutes.

Splash was a different story. When I tried to put a bit in his mouth, he backed away and eventually raised his head in anger. When I asked him to move his hips towards me, he kept his distance. When I put a rope around his belly as a first step towards trying to saddle him, he took off like a rocket, kicking and bucking his way around the pen.

I worked with Splash for about two hours, looking for even the slightest sign of a breakthrough. Eventually, we reached an uneasy truce—no trust but an end to hostilities. In the end, he gave up and decided that fighting with me wasn't worth his time. He'd made his point.

He stopped bucking and putting himself in danger. He began to do what I asked him to do without overreacting. "Let's get this over with," he seemed to be saying. That's not much of a breakthrough, and it's certainly not openness to a relationship.

Splash had a lifetime of bad habits that were almost impossible to undo. Most revolved around him over-reacting to the slightest request. He didn't care if he hurt other people. He didn't care if he crashed into a fence or knocked himself over. He was determined to get his own way no matter what.

For years, those habits had worked for him. No one ever rode him because if they tried, he'd buck them off. No one tried to force him to go somewhere he didn't want to go. No one ever even looked in his mouth. He'd just been passed from one owner to another. Along the way, he'd missed out on so much.

His life could have been different.

At his core, however, Splash was afraid. Afraid of letting someone else get close. Afraid of what it would cost him to let someone else help him or lead him. And those fears ruled his life and his interactions with others.

I didn't want to take anything from Splash. I didn't want to dominate him or bend him to my will. I wanted to offer him peace and a release from his fears. I wanted him to experience, even if for a few moments, what a trusting relationship could be like. I wanted him to have a life and future free of fear.

Unfortunately, I was likely the last person to ride Splash.

Before I got in the saddle, I called out to my friend Charlie, who had been keeping a close eye on us, and had him ride Hansom into the round pen. I wanted Charlie and Hansom nearby to keep an eye on things.

Thankfully, things ended on a quiet note. Because horses are social animals, the presence of Hansom seemed to put Splash on his best behavior, at least for a while.

But I told Splash's owners afterward that no one should ever ride him again. It pained me to tell them that. I wanted to get through, but he would not let me in. And he'd become a danger.

The most difficult part about Splash is that he was good at fooling people. When we started, he stood in the center of a round pen as if he didn't have a care in the world. He was perfectly sweet and calm and likeable—as long as everything went his way.

Even with all my experience, Splash was a handful for me. A less experienced rider would likely have lost control of him, which could have led to both the rider and the horse being hurt.

Still, Splash served as a reminder of the importance of the work we're doing. He'd never learned the basics—how to recognize boundaries, how to listen, how to think about someone else instead of himself. Instead, he'd been allowed to develop bad habits that made him explosive and unsafe.

Now he's out of options. If I'd gotten to him earlier, perhaps things would have been different. His life could have been so much different.

One more thing before we wrap up this chapter. Never break something unless you are willing to fix it afterwards. And never tear someone down unless you are willing to help them put things back together. Otherwise you've failed as a leader.

There are people who are happy where they are. They don't aspire to anything better. They are a bit like Splash and have figured out how to get by. They are fine as long as you don't push them. They'll even do what you ask them to do, as long as give them enough space.

They may not be willing or able to make the changes needed to improve their lives. The cost might just be too high. The pain of getting better is too much for them.

But if they want to get better, you, as a mentor and leader, have to be willing to stick with them even when it is hard. And you have to take steps to make sure they are safe as they work through the pain of getting better.

Not long ago I noticed one of my horses was getting lame. There was something wrong with one of his feet that needed my attention. He could not talk to me and tell me what was going on.

I needed to take some time to figure out what was happening. Was a stone caught in his shoe? Did he have a bruise of his hoof? Did he have an injury or was something else going on? I looked him all over and didn't see anything obvious.

I called the vet and had him take a closer look. He had my horse lift his foot and started putting pressure on his hoof, while I stood by, reassuring my horse that things were going to be all right. Before long, the vet hit the spot. A light touch on one area of the hoof caused the horse to react as if he'd been stabbed. There was an abscess on his hoof that needed to be drained before the infection spread.

Now my horse was not thrilled. All he knew was that we were hurting him. He wanted us to go away and leave him alone, not knowing that would make things worse. Instead we took our time and reassured him that things were going to be all right.

As I held my horse, the vet slowly pared away the hoof to get at the abscess. Then he drained it, rinsed it out, and packed it with a bandage to keep it from reinfection. We covered his hoof to protect it while it healed.

That's how leadership works. You don't just lance a sore spot and then walk away. You take your time. You make sure people feel safe and you deal with hard things. Then you stick with them until things get better.

Looking Back

In this chapter, we talked about the need for honest communication, especially when it comes to difficult topics. We learned what to do and what not to do when things don't go the way we planned. Most importantly, we learned how to earn the right to be heard.

A Few Key Points

- Always tell the truth.
- Go slow and earn trust one step at a time.
- Never overreact. Remain calm and in control.
- Remember the long-term goals.
- Don't break something unless you are willing to fix it.

Some Questions to Consider

1) What are some ways you can apply these principles in your workplace?
2) Is there someone in your life who reminds you of Splash? How can you start to get through to them?
3) Most of us have tried to confront someone about a problem, only to see things blow up. Looking back, can you identify a time that's happened in the past and how you might could have approached things differently?
4) What went through your mind when you read about the story of Nava Rose? As a leader, what do you do when you get stuck and someone just doesn't get it?
5) Have you ever had to let go of someone like Splash? How did you make that decision? What was the tipping point?
6) Can you name three ways you can improve the way you communicate?
7) Which of these principles would be hardest for you to apply?
7) What do you know at the end of this chapter that you did not know at the beginning?

Looking Ahead

The most important thing a mentor can do is capture the "want-to" of the people we lead. In the next chapter, we'll talk about the process of getting people to want to do the right thing and how to help them catch a vision of something greater than themselves.

Chapter 3

LEARNING TO SERVE

Sometimes when I'm speaking to a group of people, I'll give them a glimpse of some of the things my horse Hansom has learned.

Before the talk begins, he and I will walk around, greeting people as they file in. I'll be in the saddle and will shake hands and chat with people and occasionally pose for a picture or two. Almost no one will notice that there's no bridle on Hansom. He and I are perfectly in tune and I can tell him where to go or what to do with a bit of pressure from one of my knees.

Hansom and I have spent several years working to get to the point where whatever happens, he'll remain calm and composed and will look to me if he has a question. We are completely at ease. And that means it is safe for us to walk together in a crowd of people.

That sense of ease was the result of thousands of hours of working together. It wasn't easy. And we hit some bumps along the way.

When we first started out, Hansom made a great deal of progress in a short period of time. He's a fast learner, always gives good effort and could usually quickly master whatever I asked him to do. Then he hit a bump and began to slow down. Something seemed off.

I'd set up a new task for him to do —something like learning to lay down and then sit up or to carry me when he was blindfolded. He'd finish the task, but he never looked confident in what he was doing.

Instead, he was nervous. No matter how well he did, Hansom's body language was off. Even though we were making progress, I decided to slow down and start paying close attention. I had to see what was actually happening before I could try to make things better.

Before long, I noticed he was holding his breath whenever I asked him to do something new.

I realized he didn't believe I had confidence in him. That led him to become hesitant—so hesitant he was not living up to his abilities. He had the capability to succeed, but his lack of confidence was holding him back.

We needed to take a step back and spend some time working on his confidence. As his trainer, I needed to take an approach that would help Hansom continue to improve his skills while building his confidence and his trust in me.

So, we slowed down and took some of the pressure off. I'd give him a direction and encourage him as he worked through the process. If he needed some correction or coaching, I'd do that, but for the most part I let him work things out on his own.

We took our time and the more he practiced, the better he got. The better he got, the more his confidence and trust in me grew. He was no longer holding his breath, afraid of making a mistake. He could move on with the assurance that I believed in him.

He's not alone. Most horses—and most people—will do better when they know someone believes in them. When they know their worth doesn't depend on how well they perform. They won't be punished for every mistake. They don't have to be perfect in order to be valued.

But that kind of belief is hard to come by. Most of us are concerned about self-preservation—and will do almost anything to avoid running afoul of our boss or being seen as at fault when something goes wrong.

We fear that if we fail, we will be reprimanded, or we will lose the respect of those around us. We think our place in the world depends solely on how we perform. So, we hold our breath and try to pretend that everything is fine. That works for a while, but it can keep us—and those we lead—from reaching our full potential.

The way to get past that is to build trust and confidence. That takes a long time.

A leader may tell her people she believes in them. But few people will believe her at first. It takes a long time for a leader to gain the trust of their people and convince them their leader has their best interests at heart. Once a leader gets that kind of trust, however, their people will be highly motivated.

"People don't run through brick walls for companies," says my friend, Lisa Bahash, a longtime business executive in the automotive business. "They run through bricks walls for people. For their co-workers. For people they trust. For people who have their back."

We build that kind of trust through a slow, steady process.

One tool to help with that process is called SERVE. It's for observing and testing our relationships with others and resolving conflicts when those relationships hit a rough patch.

The process has five steps:

- Seeing
- Enforcing
- Reflecting
- Validating
- Excelling

Seeing comes first. I had to see what was happening with Hansom before I could figure out how to help him. You can't change, improve, or build something unless you see if first.

The second step, **Enforcing**, refers to setting consistent boundaries and acting in a predictable manner. With Hansom, I had to stop what we were doing and go back a few steps. I broke my requests into small pieces and set out a routine where he could repeat each step until he knew what I wanted and could perform the tasks with confidence. I didn't let him move on to the next step until he had mastered the previous one.

Reflecting, the third step, is all about listening—both with my ears and my actions. Working with Hansom, I paid close attention to his every step, making sure he knew exactly what he was expected to do. I kept an eye out for nervousness and signs he was holding his breath. And I stood nearby, every step of the way.

The fourth step, **Validate**, means showing the people who follow me the big picture, persuading them to follow my vision, and recognizing them when they move in the right direction. As we went along, I had to communicate clearly with Hansom, encouraging him to keep trying and making sure to reward him every time he did the right thing.

Excel, the fifth step, is offering approval to people for right choices and pushing them to get even better. For Hansom this mean hours and hours of repetition without rushing. I remained on the lookout to recognize and reward him when he did well. Every step of the way, I praised him and assured that he had my approval.

All five steps depended on time, clear communication, and consistent action. And, in the case of Hansom, the process began by focusing on the tasks I was asking him to perform.

Leaders—especially less-experienced leaders—sometimes believe their first priority is to build strong relationships with the people they supervise before they can push them to excel. They focus on relationship first, task second. That's a mistake.

This approach assumes that good relationships between a leader and their team are based on how we feel about each other. The assumption is that if a leader acts in a friendly manner, the people on their team will be more likely to do what the leader tells them to do. But what we do matters more than how we feel.

While a leader must always treat people with respect, strong relationships are best built when a leader sets clear and consistent boundaries and expectations for team members. When that happens, everyone knows what they are supposed to do, what the goals of the team are, and how they are supposed to conduct themselves. By doing so, the leader creates a healthy environment where everyone can flourish.

Let me give you an example.

For more than 30 years, I ran Miracle Mountain Ranch, a Western-style youth camp in Spring Creek, Pennsylvania, a rural community about an hour outside of Erie. During the summers, we'd hire college students to serve as counselors. They'd watch over the kids in the bunkhouses, take them swimming and horseback riding, and lead camp activities like crafts and archery.

Every summer, without fail, a few counselors would start the week by trying to befriend all the campers in their cabin. When camp started, they greeted each camper with a smile and helped them move in. The counselors told the campers they were just here to love them and help them have a good week. They're going to be so happy and everyone get along just perfectly.

Unfortunately, these counselors would never tell the campers the rules or set boundaries on that that first day. They'd never tell the campers what was expected of them. You can guess what happened next.

By Wednesday, the counselors would be screaming at the campers because they're running all over the place. These counselors thought that leading their cabin meant building a relationship first and worrying about tasks and boundaries later.

Other counselors also wanted the kids to have a good time and feel loved and cared for, but they set clear boundaries. These counselors went over the most important rules with the kids and put a little fear of God in them on the first day. When one of the campers tested the rules, the counselor enforced them firmly. By Wednesday, the campers had fallen into a routine, knew what they were expected to do and were having a great time—because the counselors had set up an environment that allowed the campers to thrive.

Both types of counselors had good intentions. Both wanted their campers to have a memorable week at camp. Both cared about the campers they were leading.

Yet the counselor who invested in relationships first ended up spending the whole week running ragged because their campers had never been told what was expected of them. Their campers had a terrible time because all week their counselor was yelling at them. The counselors who set the rules early, on the other hand, were able to sit back and watch their campers have the time of their lives.

That's why I spend so much time focusing on clear communication and boundaries when I teach about leadership, especially in the early sessions. They are the tools we use to build healthy relationships and a culture that allows everyone to thrive.

Not long ago, I was asked to speak to house parents at a boarding school for troubled children. These are kids who are not able to live with their parents, either because something has gone wrong at home with the parents or the children have some kind of behavioral or emotional problem.

I told the house parents the single most important thing they needed to remember is that the children needed consistency. While they need structure too, the kids needed to know that structure is consistent and safe. That's the key to building trust and stability.

One other thing to remember.

Nothing about leadership is easy. Often leadership is a confusing, messy process. You can't just say, "This is what I want. These are the rules." People don't work that way. It often takes time and repetition for people to understand what you want. And along the way, you will get frustrated. That's when you need to take a deep breath, clear your head, and get back to work.

Not long ago, one of my colleagues at Leaders by HEART told me she was at the end of her rope with someone she supervised. No matter what she tried, the other person just could not do what she wanted.

"I hate leadership," she said. I looked at her and said, "That's a lie."

She liked leadership when it was easy. We all do. She, like any other leader, liked it when someone else did what she asked them to do. She liked it when she came up with a plan, shared it with her team, and watched it come to life.

What she hated is failed leadership that does not get results.

As leaders, we hate leadership when it's frustrating, when it costs us more than we think it should. When we have to stick with someone who isn't getting it. When it requires us to grow and stretch. When we have to change in order to lead the people on our team.

Like most people, we want the biggest results for the least amount of effort. We want results that don't cost us anything. That's what my colleague wanted. But leadership is never easy, even when it looks effortless.

As I said earlier, when I'm talking to a crowd, I'll often pair Hansom with another, untrained horse, so people can see the difference between the two. I'll walk into the round pen and ask Hansom to do a fairly complex task that is difficult for horses to do, like standing with all four legs on a small box.

I'll tap or point and Hansom will do what I've asked as if it's the most natural thing in the world. Then I'll make the same request of the untrained horse. That horse will look at me like I'm crazy. They'll have no idea how to do what I've asked them to do. So, the horse will go around the box, try to jump over it, just about everything except stand on it.

If I want a horse—or an employee, student, or team member—to do a complex task, I've got to invest a lot of time with them.

I've got to break down the task into small parts and teach them one part at a time. I can't just talk to them, but I have to show them how to do what I want and why it matters. And I've got to give them the time they need to be comfortable with and master the tasks I've assigned.

You can't rush this.

If I want a horse to stand on a box, I break the training down to a series of small tasks. I start by teaching the horse how to follow my lead. I attach a rope to their bridle and start walking, stopping along the way to make sure the horse is keeping pace while also putting enough space between us so we're not stepping over each other.

I don't pull on the rope much, just enough tension so the horse knows it's time to move. After a while, the horse will learn to pick up my cues and move without even that tension.

Then I have the horse step over a piece of plywood until they feel comfortable having the wood under their feet. After that, we'd move on to putting a small box by the fence, teaching the horse to step over it, and then to stand on it.

When we were done, I could put the box in the middle of the round pen, give the signal and the horse would walk over and stand on it.

That one simple act, which looks effortless when Hansom does it, is a result of hundreds of hours of work. At each step, I made sure he heard me, he'd mastered that specific task, been rewarded, had time to rest, and that he felt validated and full of confidence.

These same principles of breaking a new task into manageable pieces, working on mastering one step at a time, and offering praise when they get things right, can be applied when working with people.

These principles work if we are willing to put in the time. If we remember that just because we say something once doesn't mean the people who work for us will understand what we want. We have to realize that it's going to take time for the people who work for us to understand, accept, and finally embrace what we want them to do.

Perhaps you are at the point my colleague was recently. You've been working hard and the people who work for you just don't get it. And you are ready to throw in the towel.

Take a deep breath. Leadership can be frustrating and tiring. It's never easy. And it's okay to say, this is not working. Once you admit that, however, it's time to take a long hard look to see why things aren't working.

Often, it's because the people who work for you don't understand what you want. If that's the case, you have to keep telling them what you want. Repeat the message as often as you can. Be as clear as possible. You may need to ask people to repeat what you've told them or to say it back to you in their own words to make sure it's clear in their minds.

Now, even when people understand what you want them to do, they may not buy in right away. It's still going to take time. You're going to have to convince them that doing what you want will have some benefit to them. You have to convince them that your ideas are worth their commitment. They won't buy into a project just to please you or because it's your pet project. They have to understand why it is worth their time.

Remember that people are going to test you, especially if you are in a new leadership role. They want to know how much they have to give in order to get your approval. They want to know if you mean what you say. Will you reward them when they do a good job? Will you value them or will you claim all the credit for yourself? And will you enforce the boundaries and goals you set?

If you validate the right things, eventually people are going to say, "Now I'm getting it." When that happens, try to catch them in the act. Reward them for forward motion and small successes. Soon those small success will snowball into good habits as they gain more confidence and more momentum.

Finally, be willing to listen when people disagree with you or when they don't understand what you want.

Let's circle back to the SERVE process I talked about earlier in this chapter.

The first step, **Seeing**, is perhaps the most important and the most time consuming because it is complicated.

For starters, no two people ever see the same thing. They each see from their own point of view, which often reveals a different angle to the situation.

It's much like the old story of the blind men who run into an elephant. Each feels a different part of the elephant and comes away with a different impression. The one who touches the elephant's trunk comes away believing that the elephant is like a snake. The one who touches the elephant's leg, thinks it is like a tree. The one who touches its ears thinks the elephant is like a giant fan. None of them has the whole truth.

To get the whole picture, we need everyone to share their point of view. We should not be surprised when other people have a different perspective. As leaders, we should gather as many points of view as possible, so we know where our people are coming from.

We have to work together to get on the same page. The process of doing that causes stress. It puts stress on our values. It puts stress on our priorities. It puts stress on people and their relationships.

When that happens, most people will look for a way out. They'll avoid the stress and try to pretend it doesn't exist. Or they will lash out in order to protect themselves. They'll feel their backs are up against a wall and refuse to give an inch. Before long, a small conflict has become a stalemate.

To avoid this, we have to tread lightly at the beginning and avoid backing people in the corner. Instead, we focus on getting people to move in the right direction. That's the key to constant improvement and good decision making—getting people moving forward rather than standing still or going backward.

Getting people moving often requires a great deal of communication. People won't move in the right direction if they don't know where they are supposed to go or if you back them into a corner. They can't know where they are supposed to go if we withhold information from them. They need to know our expectations, the criteria we are using to make decisions, and our ultimate goal.

Give them that information and then they will know where to go.

The second step—**Enforcing**— comes after people start moving.

We watch to see whether or not people choose to move in the right direction. We observe their attitudes. Are they moving because they want to or because they have to? Do they treat their colleagues well? Are they confident or timid?

If we see movement in the right direction, then we validate that movement. We tell people that they are doing the right thing. If a problem comes up, we still try to validate the person and looks for points of agreement. Our first response when a conflict comes up should be to listen and make sure the person knows they are being listened to.

One technique for making people feel heard is to reply to their comment by saying, "If I'm hearing you right…" followed by a restatement of what they said. This is the third step in the process—**Reflecting** what we see back to those we lead.

This is followed closely by the fourth step—**Validating**, which is the process of focusing on what is going right. We don't often do this well.

A person will make four points in the middle of a meeting and instead of focusing on the three points we agree with, we immediately jump to the one we disagree with. This shuts off the conversation.

If, instead, we tell the person what we agree with, then we have a starting point for a further conversation. Validating what people say makes it safe for the conversation to continue. It lets everyone know they are being rewarded for some consensus. It encourages consensus without being all-or-nothing.

Many meetings drag out because we don't pause and identify the things that we agree upon. Many negotiations fail because we don't take time to acknowledge what we have in common. We build consensus and relationship one step at a time and always are trying to go deeper in relationship and performance.

With every step along the way, we build a little more trust. Remember, there is a difference between submission and trust. An employee—or a horse—may submit to you, even if they don't trust you. They might do what you say, but they will do it begrudgingly because they don't trust our decision making.

People don't need to have their hands held. But people that are doing something new—a new project or product—need affirmation that what they are doing is worthwhile.

And they need to know how to measure success. That's the final stage—**Excelling**.

The point of this process is to help move in the right direction by making healthy decisions that lead to better outcomes, more production, and more trust.

Our people need to know they're on the right path, what the next step is in front of them, and that their leader will be there if they need help or direction.

The SERVE process isn't a one-way street. Team members are also watching their leaders and evaluating us. And we should welcome their feedback.

Recently, I had a discussion with my crew about how things were going. They've been watching while we have been on the road, giving presentations and leading training sessions. The crew that travels with me plays a key role in the presentations, often behind the scenes. They take care of all the small details so I can focus in my presentations and giving my full attention to the people that come to hear me speak.

The crew gave some pretty blunt advice. They wanted me to be clearer in my directions to them. "Don't be afraid to lead us," they said. "Don't be vague. Be clear but not mean." It was hard to hear, but important.

Like many leaders, I can get so caught up in the big picture that I don't pay attention to the people around me or the small details that shape their work lives. They can't excel if I am vague or if I act as if their questions are an annoyance.

I need to show my team that I too am committed to excellence. I can't lead them if I don't practice what I preach.

Looking Back

In this chapter, we talked about a 5-step process for helping those we mentor to move from business as usual to excellence and for building a culture of excellence.

Those steps are:

- Seeing
- Enforcing
- Reflecting
- Validating
- Excelling

Questions for Applying the SERVE MODEL

Seeing

1. Do I see and define the end goal?
2. How well do I assess and address the present?
3. How well do I define and communicate the steps to the end goal?
4. Do I prioritize my expectations to others?
5. Do I recognize and reward forward motion?

Enforcing

1. Does my yes mean yes?
2. Does my no mean no?
3. Do I communicate a yes in every no?
4. Do I define and defend boundaries?
5. Do I empower others through being clear?

Reflect

1. Do I listen louder than I speak?
2. Do I consistently listen with my eyes?
3. Do I listen with my feet?
4. Do I make others feel heard?
5. Do I listen with intention and deliberation?

Validate

1. Do I continually define the big picture?
2. Do I clearly define the next step?
3. Do I consistently recognize and reward right movement?
4. Am I a bridge builder, not a gap maker?
5. Do I take things apart without putting them together?

Excel

1. Do I know 10 ways I can show my people how improve?
2. Do my people value my approval?
3. Do I clearly approve good work?
4. Am I a hope giver?
5. Am I a life giver?

Looking Ahead

These first four chapters have focused on how to become a better leader—how to set appropriate boundaries, how to earn trust, how to talk about hard things, and how to pursue excellence. In the next few chapters, we'll focus more closely on the process of mentoring—how to help those who follow us become leaders in their own right.

Chapter 4

TRAIL BOSS

Let's start this chapter with a review of what we've learned so far.

In chapter 1, we talked about the big picture—how to create a culture of sound decision-making through a pursuit of excellence. We met my friend Ryan, who looked around his company and realized that despite its business success, something was missing.

In chapter 2, we looked at some of the pushback that comes when a leader tries to set boundaries and challenges the status quo. We met Buddy the horse, who'd suffered from benign neglect for years before his new owners took a painful but necessary step to change the course of his life.

In chapter 3, we focused on the idea that leadership involves winning people's hearts. We can't force others to do what we want to do, but we can help them learn how to want to do the right thing. We also met Splash, a horse who decided that going his own way was more important than saving his own life, and Nava Rose, a horse who changed my life by teaching me that I wasn't quite the brilliant leader I thought I was.

In chapter 4, we talked about the importance of building trust and investing in relationships. We discussed some of the skills and techniques I have learned to build healthy, trusting relationships. And we met my horse Hansom, who struggled with confidence when he was younger but is now a trusted, confident companion.

The focus on those four chapters was on how to become a good leader, someone who creates an environment that helps the people on their team succeed.

Now I want to talk about mentoring, which is the process by which we teach others how to become leaders. I would argue it's the most important step of being a leader. After all, we all know of successful companies, sports teams, churches or other organizations that fall apart after a beloved leader leaves.

There's even a condition known as "Founder's Syndrome," which describes what happens when an organization's whole culture is built around a leader's strengths and weaknesses, rather than a heathy culture with strong practices. Things appear great until something goes wrong with the leader, then everything falls apart.

We also know of leaders who do well with one team, company, or organization, but then fall flat on their faces when they move to a new job. It's often because they don't know how to adapt to a new situation and new people. Their leadership skills are limited because they only know how to lead one particular group in one particular setting.

Mentoring requires learning how to broaden our leadership skills, so that we know how to lead a wide variety of people. We adapt our style to the needs of our people. That doesn't mean we compromise our principles or our commitment to excellence. Instead, it means that we become flexible and realize that what we've done in the past won't always work in the future.

I've learned this lesson the hard way over the past 40 years, by trial and error and slowly discovering a set of principles that, when applied with determination and commitment, can yield consistent growth.

As we talk about these principles, I want to tell you a bit more of my story and why I have come to believe so strongly in mentorship. I've told much of this in a previous book, *Life Lessons from a Horse Whisperer*, but it bears repeating.

The gist of it is this: my career as a leader and mentor almost ended before it started.

In the early 1980s, my father-in-law Dale asked me to take over as director of the Miracle Mountain Ranch. He'd run the camp since the 1960s and was ready to step down. I can't say how honored I was when he asked me to take over as the camp's leader, how much I felt I owed Dale, and how important it was to continue his legacy. Meeting him literally changed my life.

I'd come from a difficult home and while I'd had great success at a young age, my life felt empty and without purpose. I knew how to train horses, but I was rough around the edges when I arrived at

Miracle Mountain. I did not know how to lead other people or love them. Or how to let them love me.

Coming to the camp was like joining a new family. Dale embraced me—literally. He was one of the first men ever to hug me and show me unconditional love. He taught me there was more to life than money and success. I also met Dale's daughter, Melodie, there and the two of us eventually fell in love, married, and decided to work at the camp.

When Dale named me as his successor, this caused some problems. Some of the older staff thought they'd been passed up for the top job, which went to this young outsider. But at the time, that was the least of my worries.

Enrollment was down, in part because our reputation had been tarnished after a disagreement between my father-in-law and a former ministry partner turned into a public feud. The conflict ruined years of trust at local churches, meaning they sent fewer kids to our camp. Lower attendance meant fewer camp fees, which meant our revenue dropped.

Running a small nonprofit camp is a challenge in the best of times. Money's always tight and you have to pinch every penny. But in a crisis, a decline in revenue can threaten your organization's survival.

When I became the camp's director, we were essentially broke. We barely had enough money to keep the lights on, heat the buildings, or even buy toilet paper. I used to joke that we might have to go back to using corn cobs in the outhouses.

We had no money, little trust among the staff members, and no easy way to move forward. It would have been easy to give up. But we had time on our hands. And a staff who, even if they didn't trust me completely, believed in our mission. So, we got to work.

The ranch's property was heavily forested, so we started by chopping firewood. We cut down trees, chopped them into logs, and stacked the wood everywhere. We used that to heat our essential buildings and shut down the others.

I picked out an axe and worked side by side with our staff. As we worked together, we talked about our mission and their hopes and dreams for the ranch and for their lives. The whole team worked in the wet and the cold. We laughed together. We ate together. We played together—watching movies and eating popcorn. We built a community.

As we did all of that, I watched. I saw who pitched right in and helped out and who stood back. I watched to see which staff would take charge when we hit problems and who stopped when challenges arose. I watched to see who was growing and showing new abilities and who was stuck.

At first, all we did was keep the camp alive. Then we began to improvise and try new things. As a new director, I'd been hesitant to change anything in those first two years. But when it became clear that what we had been doing wasn't working, we had to change.

Dale was great during this time. He had stayed on as an advisor and board member and saw the toll that trying to keep the camp afloat was taking. He and other board members came to me one day and asked if I wanted them to close down the camp, sell the property, and call it a day. "No," I said. "Let's give it one more year. But things will have to change." Dale agreed and gave me his blessing to do things differently.

His belief in me worked wonders. He freed me up to try new things, and, in turn, I could do the same for my staff without fear of letting him down. We now had the freedom to improvise and be creative. And just as important, we had the freedom to fail. If we tried something new and it didn't work, we'd move on the next new things. We had nothing to lose.

In this process, our staff learned how to make do with very little. I'd drive my truck around looking for old barns that were being torn down and or were about fall over and ask the owners if we salvage any of the wood. We'd collect old nails, pound them straight, and then use that salvaged wood and the old nails to give our buildings a facelift.

When I arrived, the buildings looked tired. They were solid and well-built but dull, lacking any personality or character. Since our camp had a Western theme, I wanted the buildings to look as if they belonged in the Wild West. So, like a Hollywood director of old Western movies, we created false fronts for the buildings made out of the recycled barn wood to recreate the feel of a frontier town.

We also sold off our cattle to raise money—something Dale had been reluctant to do—and invested the money in new programs. Little by little, things got better.

At one point, I also leveled with my staff. "I don't know how to fix this," I said. "I need your help."

The temptation for leaders is to pretend we have all the answers. We think that asking for help is a sign of weakness. We are afraid to trust the people who work for us with important tasks out of fear they won't do things the way we would have done them.

But asking for help is not a sign of weakness. And the people who work for us won't learn how to grow into leaders if we don't let them fail and learn from their mistakes.

Plus, our people know if things aren't going well, so why pretend? Why not ask them to help and build something together?
Mentoring starts by realizing we need other people. That investing in them is important. It may be hard in the beginning but it pays off over the long term.

There's saying in business that you have to get the right people on the bus in the right seats—and the wrong people off the bus—in order for your business to thrive. The idea is that if you have the right people with the right skills doing the right jobs, then things will fall into place.

Maybe.

Yes, it's important that you find the right people and match them to jobs they are suited for. But sometimes the right people are already on the bus. You and they just might not realize it yet. They may need someone who can show them the way to go and help them grow and develop.

That's what we did at the ranch. I committed to the people we had and invested in them—people like Ralph McGill.

Ralph first came to the ranch as young boy over 40 years ago. He'd been thrown out of two or three other camps already. No one expected him to last long. But my father-in-law put his arm around

Ralph, told his mother that he'd be just fine, and waved as she drove off.

Though he gave my father-in-law a run for his money, Ralph eventually came to love Miracle Mountain. He had a special place in his heart for troubled campers and would often sit with them for hours, showing them that he cared and that he would still love them, no matter what they did.

When I took over, I made Ralph my right-hand man. He helped run the summer camp, organized our year-long apprentice program, and led the staff when I was not around. I would trust Ralph with my life. With his help and the help of other staff, we put the camp back on solid footing.

People saw what we were doing and began to take an interest. We rebuilt ties with the community. Attendance at summer camps grew. Parents began to trust us with their children and wanted them to experience what we offered. Our finances stabilized, and we created a solid future for the ranch.

I stepped down as director a number of years ago, but I'm happy to say that things are still going strong there. The camp outlasted my leadership tenure because of the investment I made in the people there.

People also invested in the work we were doing.

One summer, a couple came to me, looking for advice. Their son had graduated from high school but wasn't quite ready to go to college. They wondered if I'd be willing to take him on as an apprentice for year, so he could work and learn and have time to mature before heading to college. And hopefully, he could earn some credits for college through the ranch, as a kind of internship. I thought it over and talked to Melodie. We eventually agreed but with a few conditions. First, we were going to charge him for spending the year with us. There'd be some costs for housing, food, and setting up a system that would allow him to get college credit. More importantly, we wanted their son, or any apprentice we brought on, to have a sense of ownership and buy in. We wanted to make sure they were willing to pay the price of being committed. Second, we needed to find at least one other person to spend the year with us, alongside their son. We felt that if he came on his own and didn't have at least one person his age to relate with, things might go poorly. Eventually another young man signed on and joined us at the camp.

I spent a lot of time with those two young men, Dan Cooper and Greg Pike, during that first year. We took them through a program we called DISCIPLE, which had eight parts:

- **Discipline**: We ran a tight schedule, with set times for chores, meals, study and recreation, so the year had a sense of order and direction.
- **Identity**: We worked on their personal development, identifying their gifts and abilities, and helped them shore up areas of weakness, while building on their strengths.
- **Study**: We set up regular study time, teaching them academic theories, as well as principles of leadership and personal growth. Because we were a Christian camp, this also included Bible study. We wanted to teach them how to learn and to love learning.
- **Crisis**: We knew that at some point of the year, something would go wrong. Or they'd do something that needed

correction. So we gave them clear feedback and constructive criticism when things went wrong. And we also taught how to handle a crisis with grace and ingenuity.

- **Inclusion**: We taught them how to make decisions as a team, asking for their input and then walking them through the processes of evaluating options and making a wise choice.
- **Practice**: They had regular chores and practice sessions to work on their horsemanship, as well as their leadership abilities. We wanted them to learn both practical skills and management lessons.
- **Love**: We invested in them as people, communicating whenever we could that they were loved and valued. We treated them with kindness and praise along with structure.
- **Ethics**: We established clear boundaries and expectations and clearly communicated our values—honesty, trustworthiness, dependability, concern for other people, and commitment to the camp's mission.

Our investment in these young men during that year paid off. Both went on to have successful lives and careers. They paved the way for others to follow. We eventually had as many as 40 or 50 apprentices a year working at the camp, all earning college credit while learning how to be leaders.

When I left, I was thrilled that Matt Cox, who'd come to the camp as an apprentice and eventually joined the staff, was named executive director. It was a reminder that mentoring others is always worth it.

The horses at that camp also taught me about mentoring and leadership. For starters, they taught me that I was not as great a trainer or a leader as I thought I was.

I'd had a lot of success training horses and had won my share of trophies. But for the most part, the horses I worked with were high-price, talented horses that came from great bloodlines, including some of the finest Appaloosa horses in the country.

The horses at the Miracle Mountain were not prize winners. They were plain and a bit pokey. Many were older and had been donated to the camp. They were great for kids to ride but nothing to write home about. I've sometimes described them as suburban dads playing touch football in the park, while the horses from my former life were more like NFL athletes playing in front of packed stadiums.

Most of the horses at our camp were just average, especially this one horse named Peyote.

He was a nice enough horse. The kids loved him, and he was great for giving riding lessons to beginners. But he wasn't very bright or athletic. So, anything beyond beginning lesson would be more than he could handle. The same was true for most of the other horses at our ranch, with the exception of one—a pretty young mare named Ribbon. Or so I thought.

Ribbon was a lovely horse. She was athletic, talented, well-bred. I thought she could be something more than a run-of the-mill camp horse. So, I started to train her, giving her extra attention, and teaching her to do the kinds of tasks and routines that I'd taught to prize-winning horses in the past. Despite her talent, my training efforts with Ribbon failed.

She was happy with just being a camp horse and didn't have any interest in learning more. She got irritated at even the simplest tasking—swishing her tail, pinning back her ears, turning her head when I was trying to get her attention, and sending me the message that she wanted to be left alone. She'd give a little bit of effort but only a little, always satisfied with doing the bare minimum. Ribbon got the job done. But just barely. And she was never was able to tap into her potential.

Peyote, on the other hand, was a bit of a revelation. He was eager to learn and picked up new tasks quickly. He worked hard and seemed to generally like being around me. He far exceeded all of my expectation.

Before long I was taking the two of them to training events and public presentations. People took one look at Ribbon and thought she was a star. They'd wonder why on earth she was in the same pen with Peyote. Then they'd watch in amazement as he ran rings around her. It got to a point where I could direct Peyote with a nod or a simple nudge from my knee and he'd do what I asked.

Now Peyote had limits. He wasn't as physically gifted as Ribbon or other horses I'd trained. He couldn't do flying lead changes—a technique where a horse changes its lead foot mid-canter—because he lacked the athleticism to pull it off. But Ribbon, who had the physical gifts that Peyote lacked, couldn't do these kinds of changes either because she had no interest in putting forth the effort needed to learn them.

I worked for years with Peyote, who played an essential role in expanding the outreach work that eventually became Leaders by HEART. Audiences fell in love with him and were constantly surprised by the skill that plain yet lovable horse displayed. He reminded them—and me—not to be fooled by appearances.

By the time I'd gotten to the ranch, I had become a bit of a horse snob, believing that only well-bred, expensive, and beautiful horses were worth spending my time with. Peyote taught me that any horse, no matter how humble their appearance, had the potential for greatness, if a trainer was willing to invest in them.

Eventually, as word of what I was doing with Leaders by HEART spread, I began to get better horses to work with, like Spotlight, a Quarter Horse stallion who I first met in the early 2000s.

Spotlight's parents had been prize-winning horses and great things had been expected of him. When he was born, he'd inherited all of his parent's athleticism and ability, along with their calm and confident demeanor. His golden coat and white mane caught your eye.

All in all, he was the kind of horse that every trainer would love to work with—except for the fact that he was worthless, at least from a financial point of view.

On one side, he had a large, bright white spot, that, at least for breeding purposes, ruined his coat. No one would pay top dollar for a horse with that kind of aesthetic defect, despite his champion bloodlines.

By the time he was three, Spotlight had grown into a beloved, good-natured horse, but one whose life had no purpose. His owners loved to be around him because he had a delightful personality and was descended from champions. But there was no use spending anytime training him or investing in his development.

Eventually his owners, who were friends, lent Spotlight to me and later gave him to me. He became a great companion and partner in my work. He had all the best of Peyote—eager to learn, always willing to work hard—along with great athleticism. We had years of success together.

I'd often put him in a round pen with a younger or untrained horse for comparison, allowing people to see how much a well-trained horse was capable of. His calm demeanor allowed me to demonstrate the power of mentoring. I'd tie him to another horse, a technique called ponying, and allow him to lead that untrained horse around the arena. Even the most flighty or stubborn horse would soon fall in line under his close watch. Having Spotlight expanded the appeal of our training. Eventually I was able to acquire more horses like him, including my current horses, Hansom and Pistol.

Pistol, it turns out, is the most athletic and talented horse I have ever owned. His full name is French Royal Pistol. A friend teased me when I gave him that name and said I might get more than I asked for. My friend was right.

When I first got Pistol, he was, shall we say, excitable. He was very energetic and a bit anxious. He loved to run around but had an unfortunate habit of not paying attention to what he was doing. A couple times he ended up running full steam into the fence because he was so excited and not looking where he was going.

Pistol was also very sensitive, not bad tempered but sensitive and easily discouraged. He wanted so much to please me as his trainer and would get down on himself if things didn't go well. And in the early days of training, there's a lot of trial and error you just have to press through.

If I put too many boundaries on him, he'd quit. If I didn't put enough boundaries around him, he'd get insecure and anxious. He was, in short, a lot of work. In some ways, he was like a number of people I've worked with—really talented and highly-skilled people but also high strung. They can accomplish great things but take a lot of work to manage.

Most of the work I do is in public and involves a lot of traveling and constantly being in new, unfamiliar situations, surrounded by strangers. I need my horses to be a steady and calm presence in the arena, because their confidence rubs off on the other horses I work with. And I need them to pay attention to me and not their surroundings. A horse who is high maintenance or has stage fright just won't work.

By the time he was 3-years-old, I began to suspect Pistol didn't have a future with me. He's a good horse—smart, talented, eager to please, and full to the brim with athletic talent. He is probably the most talented horse I'd ever owned, but he is very emotional and not good at failing. He was always in a hurry and had no patience

The legendary basketball coach John Wooden, who led UCLA to 10 national championship in his four decades, used to say, "Be quick, but don't hurry." His wanted his team to be decisive and move quickly to do the right thing—without rushing.

Pistol was always in a rush and, as a result, he struggled. He didn't have the confidence or the patience to take things one step at a time. He was always trying to do every step all at once, as fast as he could.

I decided to put him up for sale. Because he was such a talented horse, he was worth quite a bit of money. I set a price of $50,000 on him, which I felt was a fair price. A few people came to look at him and eventually someone offered me $25,000. I decided to hang on to him to see if he would advance in his training. If that happened, perhaps someone would be willing to pay more for him.

Then I began to realize maybe Pistol wasn't the problem. Maybe it was me.

I'd grown used to working with a certain kind of horse—easy-going, even tempered, eager to please. While my horses had talent, they were never the best horses. They were over-achievers rather than star-caliber horses. They were good but not great. Their willingness to learn and the chemistry that developed between us allowed both the horses and I to excel. They were, to put it bluntly, my kind of horses.

Pistol was not. He was a star. Or at least he had the makings of star. He had great talent and potential, but he needed my help to unlock that talent and reach his potential.

It was the Ribbon problem all over again. Pistol had all kinds of untapped potential. It was up to me to help him put that talent to work. He, unlike Ribbon, was willing. But he lacked the inner confidence so many of my other horses had.

In chapter 3, I talked about how leaders have to adapt their leadership style to fit the people on their team. You can only ride one horse at a time, I often say. It's a way of reminding people that even when you have a team, each person is different. As a leader, you need to lead each person as an individual as well as the team as a whole. And you can only speak as loudly as the other person—or the horse—can hear.

Well, Pistol couldn't hear me. I wasn't training him in a way that he could understand. I was treating him like all my other horses instead of trying to match my training to his strengths. Pistol needed me to be a different kind of leader.

Now the easy thing to do would have been to move on from Pistol. It was going to take a lot of work for me to get through to him. And it was going to stretch me. I needed to learn some new skills and change my ways, which is not easy to do, especially when what I'd done in the past had worked pretty well. But good leaders don't give up on their people.

There was no guarantee things would work out with Pistol, no matter how much I tried. In order to see the training though, I had to decide whether or not Pistol was worth the effort. I had to ask myself if I was willing to change. Was I willing to invest the effort to learn the skills I needed to help Pistol grow and succeed? Did I really believe in all the things I had been teaching over the years?

It was a high-risk, high-reward situation. If the training succeeded, Pistol would reach his potential, and the combination of his physical talent with high skill level would be a great asset to the work I do. The experience of learning to lead a highly talented horse would also give me insights on what it's like to lead highly skilled but temperamental people, which is not uncommon leadership challenge.

The downside, if the training failed, would be a lot of wasted time and energy—time and energy that could have been invested in other horses and other people.

I'd like to say that I decided to take a chance on Pistol because I believed in him, and that training him would be an opportunity for the both of us to grow. But the truth is, the decision was made for me. No one would offer me what I thought Pistol was worth, so I was stuck with him.

I decided to make the best of it. That included asking for help. I called trainer friends who had worked with highly talented horses and asked for advice. I consulted experts on how to lead highly skilled people. And I looked back on what I'd done in the past to see if there were lessons or techniques that I could adapt to use for Pistol. I also took some more of my advice.

First, I closed the back door—something I often tell leaders to do. Because of my frustration in training Pistol, I wasn't 100 percent committed to him. I was ready to be rid of him and was just biding time till someone took him off my hands. I lacked commitment to see things through with Pistol. So, when he struggled, I lost faith in him. Closing the back door meant committing whole-heartedly to making this work.

We also focused on small wins, which again is part of my standard advice for leaders. "Own the small things," I tell people, "and the big things will fall into place." Good advice. So, I put it into practice.

I began to watch Pistol carefully and think about what he might be going through in the training. He was eager to please, which I realized betrayed a lack of confidence on his part. His greatest strength, his athletic speed, was turning out to be his greatest weakness. What he needed most was to slow down, both physically and emotionally. So that's where we started.

I dialed back my expectations of him. I'd expected him, with his talent, to do great things, which put tremendous pressure on both Pistol and me, as his trainer. We changed direction. I began to focus on small wins. We slowed down. I broke every task into smaller and smaller pieces, so he had less to focus on. All he had to think about was doing one small thing right, over and over again. Every time he got something right, I praised him.

Little by little, the training began to pay off. His confidence grew—and the more it grew—the more I could challenge him. After a while, he began to see that failing was all right. When he made a mistake, he didn't fall apart. Instead, he began to trust me and believe I would not give up on him. That belief helped his confidence grow.

Twenty years ago, this would not have been possible. Back then, I didn't have the patience, flexibility or time to train and invest in a horse like Pistol. I was building our business and on the road all the time. The pressure to succeed and the demands on my time would have made it hard to invest in a horse like Pistol.

I'm still busy, but I've become more aware of the importance of investing in other people. I've also realized that investing in others demands that I still grow and learn. It's not a one-way street. I'm not a fountain gushing with wisdom. I am a friend and mentor who can listen and share my experience and put those experiences to work for the benefit of others.

Not long ago, my friend Craig, an executive at an automotive supply company, found himself in a situation where things were not going the way he wanted. He and his team had been working on a new project to improve his company's products and were ready to present their findings. They'd spent months on the project and had honed their presentation to perfection.

Craig was meeting with his bosses to make a final pitch. If they approved, the project would go forward and his team's hard work would be rewarded.

Before the meeting, he was sure the project would be greenlighted. He made his pitch, laying out the reasons why the project would be a win for the company, and it went off without a hitch.

Then his bosses said no.

Craig was disappointed for his team. He hated to see all their work go down the drain. And he couldn't see why the project had been turned down. "There was no good reason for it," Craig said later.

He suspected that politics, rather than good sense, led to the decision. He walked out disappointed and frustrated, feeling the company had let a good idea go to waste. Not that he let his bosses know how he felt.

Craig nodded, accepted their decision, and gave no outwards sign of his inward disappointment. In the past, he would have stewed about the decision and been angry at work for weeks. He likely would have taken his frustration out at home.

Had Craig done so, it would have hurt him and his company. But he'd been working on improving his leadership skills, especially his ability to deal with disappointment. He'd been in the corporate world long enough to know that politics often play a role in decision making. And he also knew that sometimes good ideas get passed over.

Still, he had to go back to his team and pass on the news. How he did that would affect the team's morale and likely their performance for weeks to come. So, he sat down with them and calmly explained that the project had been shot down.

"I looked at my team and said, 'Let's regroup and move on,'" he recalled. "I told them, 'We'll file this idea away and maybe we'll get a chance to come back to it. But for now, let's move on.'" That one decision, says Craig, did the trick.

His team was still disappointed. But they didn't let their disappointment stop them or derail their work. They didn't get angry at their co-workers or stew at management. Instead, they rolled up their sleeves and got back to work. That moment was a breakthrough for Craig.

In the past, he'd taken work disagreements to heart. Every disagreement left a scar and undermined his confidence in both the company and his own abilities. Now, while he disagreed with the decision, he didn't make it personal or hold a grudge.

"People disagree in business—it happens all the time," he says. "And disagreement can be healthy. But it becomes unhealthy when you carry the baggage of the past into every discussion."

Craig was able to set aside this temporary setback and think about the big picture for himself and for his team. It would have done his team no good if they had focused on their setback. Instead they were able to move quickly to the next project. They weren't discouraged by the decision. They didn't let it change how they saw their coworkers or how they saw themselves.

A similar situation happened recently at the Little League World Series. The team from Elizabeth, New Jersey had made it all the way to Williamsport, Pennsylvania, where the Little League World Series takes place. There they lost to a team from River Ridge, Louisiana. The team from Elizabeth played well. They had done their best. But that day, the other team was just a little bit better After the game, the team's coach, Jairo Labrador, gathered the team around him and told them how proud he was of them.

"Elizabeth is so proud of you guys," he said. "It was so awesome today…. I love the way we didn't give up." He told the players he loved them. "For the rest of my life, I'm proud," he said.

Then, in a lighthearted moment, he told them one more thing. "I need you guys to help me up," he said, reaching out his hand and smiling. He'd been kneeling down and got stuck.

The coach's speech might have gone unnoticed had someone not caught it on video. It was posted online and soon went viral, watched by millions of people all over the world and making headlines everywhere.

Some people criticized the coach for being too soft on these kids, saying he congratulated them for being losers. Those critics were wrong. The team from Elizabeth was one of the best in the country. They had made it all the way to the top. Out of thousands of Little League teams in America, they were among the best. One loss did not take that away from them.

That speech reveals a core principle of the Leaders by HEART training—kindness and excellence can go hand-in-hand. You can be strong, aggressive, and compete at the top of your game and be gentle at the same time.

In order to understand this principle, however, we have to know the difference between perfection and excellence.

Perfect is fragile. It is self-centered. Its main concern is making yourself look good and never showing a moment of weakness. And it cannot last. One mistake and perfection is taken away.

Excellence is a different matter. It's about others. It's about doing your best to give other people the best you have to offer, helping them thrive, and even at times surpass their coach.

Excellence is about pushing people to do their best without leaving anyone behind. That's what we're after. Capturing the heart of the people we lead. Showing that we care enough for them to push them to be the best they can be. Showing them they matter and can perform at a high level. And believing in them—and sticking with them—till they make it happen.

Looking Back

In this chapter, we outlined eight factors that help those we lead turn into leaders.
- Discipline
- Identity
- Study
- Crisis
- Inclusion
- Practice
- Love
- Ethics

We also focused on the important difference between excellence and perfection. Perfection is always self-focused. Its main concern is about appearances and cannot be satisfied with a job well done. Excellence, on the other hand, is when we push people to become their very best and use their gifts and skill for the greatest possible good. Excellence is focused outward.

Some Questions to Consider

1) When he was leading the Miracle Mountain Ranch, things began to turn around for Lew when he able to say, "I don't have all the answers" and asked for help. Have you ever been in that situation? Did you ask for help? If now, what got in the way?

2) What you take away from the story of Ribbon and Peyote? Have you ever had a similar experience?

3) Think of a time when your boss made a decision you disagreed with — or when something you'd worked on failed. How did you respond?

4) What was your reactions to Craig's story? Is there anything that you can learn from his approach?

5) What's your definition of excellence? How does it compare to your definition of perfection? Which would you rather have, excellence or perfection?

Looking Ahead

In the next chapter, we'll talk about the privilege of leadership, why "servant leadership" is often misunderstood, and the importance of sharing credit for success.

Chapter 5

THE FOREMAN

My friend Lisa Bahash has a simple rule for leadership: When things go right, never take credit. Success, she says, is meant to be shared.

"I don't go into a meeting and say, I did this," says Lisa, a longtime auto industry executive who has turned around a number of troubled companies. "I will say my team did this, or our organization accomplished this. But I won't say that I did it."

Lisa is mostly retired now but she still coaches young leaders and serves on several corporate boards. Most of her time is devoted to helping leaders understand leadership is privilege, not a right. "Leadership is a privilege given to me by others, for the good of the organization," she says.

Leadership, in other words, means being responsible for the welfare of others. It's not a thing to be taken lightly. If a leader succeeds, the people around her will flourish. If she fails, the people around her suffer the consequences.

The best way for a team to succeed, she believes, is to have a leader who empowers other people to do their best. No leader can succeed on their own, Lisa says. So, a leader has to help others grow, develop and take charge of things.

At the same time, a leader has to lead. They have to show people the way to go. But they can't manage every step their team makes. It's difficult balance.

A leader has to be in charge and set the course for a team while not micromanaging. They have to have a steady hand on the reins without holding on too tight. They have to be in charge without hogging the spotlight.

"I don't like the term 'servant leadership,'" she says. "I think that's a bunch of malarkey. But leadership is a privilege. I keep myself in check by remembering that."

For Lisa, the whole point of being a leader is to help others grow and succeed. It means making a long-term investment in the growth and development of other people.

"Leadership is an obligation to do the best you can for your organization in a way that benefits not just the company but all the people who make up the company," she says. "You have an obligation to develop your people— helping those people grow, helping manage their careers, helping them develop their potential, and honoring that relationship."

A quick note. The term "servant leadership" is often used in Christian circles as a way of pointing leaders to the example of Jesus, who, despite being the Son of God, did not seek power for its own sake, but instead gave his life of the benefit of others. He was willing to literally wash the feet of those who followed him and considered his disciples his friends.

But humility is not weakness. Or inaction.

At times, "servant leadership" is misinterpreted to mean a passive leader who is afraid to take charge or show people what needs to be done, instead of seeing a servant leader as one who lives their life for the benefit of others and the greater good. I agree with the latter, not the former.

This is an essential part of Leaders by HEART. It's why we do what we do. We want to show leaders how they can capture the heart of those around them—so people follow leaders because they want to, not because they have to. So, people invest their whole selves in the mission of the organization and, in doing so, thrive.

This is, as we've talked about, not easy. It requires trust and excellence on both sides. A leader has to be skilled and have a vision for how everyone on their team can thrive, not just the leader or the organization. They do this by providing strong, steady, consistent leadership and investment in their people. In other words, by mentoring the people who work for them and looking out for their best interest.

In the last chapter, we talked at length about how to invest in other people and why that matters. And we talked about the importance of leaders admitting they have to rely on other people in order to succeed. Now I want to talk about how this works on a day-to-day basis in my world.

I can't do what I do—the horse training, the speaking, the traveling, the employee training, the mentoring—without a whole host of people who work behind the scenes. My team sets up the pens, cares for the horses, sells books, organizes volunteers, and keeps an eye on me when my attention is focused on a horse in the round pen.

I have confidence when I walk in the round pen because I know they have my back. They are talented, well-trained, and trusted friends and colleagues. We've spent thousands of hours together building trust and confidence in one another, as well as building skills and knowledge.

Let's go back to Splash, an older, troubled horse I told you about in chapter 3. Splash, if you recall, was trouble. On the outside, he appeared to be a nice horse—calm, healthy, good natured, mature—just the kind of horse to take on a nice, long ride in the country.

At 14, he exuded confidence and well-being. Except when you put a saddle on him. Or asked him to do something he didn't want to do. Then Splash exploded, bucking all over the round pen, with no concern for his own safety or the safety of those around him. He was a handful and it took all my effort and concentration to keep both Splash and I from getting into trouble.

After about an hour and a half working with Splash, he and I came to a compromise. He would tolerate my presence, as long as I did not push him too far. I spent some time testing that compromise, making sure that Splash would live up to his side of the agreement Eventually, I figured he was safe enough to take for a short ride.

Had I been on my own, I never would have gotten on Splash's back, but I was not alone. My friend Charlie was there. Kami, one of my longtime assistants, was also there and was keeping an eye on me and on Hansom as he grazed on the lawn outside the round pen. They were on standby, just in case I needed them. They are well trained and know exactly what to do if things start to get out of hand.

Right before I climbed into the saddle, I called out to Charlie. "Why don't you bring Hansom in here," I said in a calm voice while making a few final adjustments to Splash's saddle.

To folks in the audience, it sounded like I was just making conversation with Charlie or asking him to join me on a nice leisurely ride. No hint of panic or worry in my voice. While I was not panicked or worried, I was concerned—and because of that, I wanted Charlie and Hansom nearby.

Hansom and I have worked together for years. He is an old pro when it comes to dealing with difficult horses. He's had years of practice.

Early on in his training, I began to pony him with other horses. This is something I had done with all the horses who work with me on a regular basis as part of their training.

As I talked about in chapter 5 with Spotlight, I take a length of rope and tie one end to the saddle of my horse, the other end to the bridle of another horse. Then my horse will lead the other horse around the pen, arena, or practice facility where we are working.

Often, we're doing that with an untrained horse, who may not take kindly to being tied to another horse. Sometimes they bite, shove my horse with their shoulder, or bolt ahead of my horse. But I've trained my horses not to react in that situation.

They don't retaliate when another horse misbehaves. Instead they are calm and steady—and their calm and steady presence keeps the other horse in line. In the process, my horse teaches the other horse how to behave and be responsible when carrying a rider.

My horse's confidence gives the other horse the confidence to do the right thing, or at least to pretend to do the right thing while my horse is watching. Sometimes we all have to practice doing the right thing. And most of us try to be on our best behavior when someone else is watching.

Right after I called, Charlie began walking at a brisk but unhurried pace towards Hansom. Kami doubled-checked Hansom's saddle and reins. As soon as Charlie was settled aboard him, she swung the pen gate open and let them in.

Once I saw that Charlie was moving, I climbed into the saddle and went for a ride with Splash. It was a little like going on a roller coaster ride; I knew I was safe, but things had the potential to get exciting.

I wanted Splash to take a nice, easy walk around the pen. He tried to speed up and get much closer to the side of the pen than I was comfortable with. He wanted to show he was in charge. And, if he was lucky, maybe bang me against the fence as payback for making him work so hard.

I had to rein him in and not let him get a full head of steam. Just when I got the feeling that Splash might get unruly, Hansom pulled up next to us.

Immediately a sense of calm and control filled the round pen. Splash became a different horse. He settled down to very comfortable trot, and we took a nice jaunt around the pen before we called it a day. No one got hurt, and we avoided too much excitement.

None of that would have been possible had I not spent years working with Hansom, Charlie and Kami—building their skills and awareness and our relationship. They knew exactly what to do when I needed it. I didn't have to micromanage them. I knew they'd get the job done, no questions asked.

Not only that, if something had gone wrong in that pen, I had the utmost confidence they would do the right thing to keep the horses, the audience, and even their boss safe. They aren't just good followers. They are great team members and leaders in their own right.

Someday they may even surpass me. But that's the goal. To train them up and watch them succeed. And maybe even once in a while watch them bail you out when things go wrong. In fact, that's how Charlie and I came to work together.

We'd know each other for years. He and his family had supported our work and hosted some leadership training and horsemanship events that I'd led. And when he was trying to become a better leader in his horse dentistry business, I'd coached him.

We were friends, and I enjoyed our time together. I was able to help him, both in his leadership skills and his horse training. Then I broke my leg. Charlie dropped everything to come to my aid and help our work at Leaders by HEART stay afloat when I was out of commission.

Here's what happened.

I was doing a round pen event with a horse that had never been ridden before in Jackson, Tennessee, about two hours west of Nashville. I'd done several events in Jackson in the past and had a number of friends and several churches there that supported my work.

The event was supposed to be held outside at the fairgrounds not far from the city center. When I arrived that morning, however, the skies were filled with clouds and rain was in the forecast. Since I've been doing this work for years, I always have a backup plan. In this case, there was a large exhibit hall at the fairgrounds with plenty of clear space for me to work. So, we decided to move the event inside.

This was nothing new. Over the years, I'd done events inside with wooden floors, carpeted floors, concrete floors—you name it. And I always have a number of alternate programs in my back pocket, just in case.

I could not ride an untrained horse inside a fairground building. That was a non-starter. It would not be fair to the horse to put them in a new environment, where the footing might be uncertain and they might feel panicked or worried because of the sounds echoing around them. That kind of stress could put them at risk. There's no way they can learn how to listen to me as their training when their mind is filled with worries and distractions. So, I switched to a program with one my own horses.

We'd made the decision early on, so I had time to get my horse prepared. The building was big enough for me to drive my truck and trainer inside, so we pulled up, parked, and unloaded without much difficulty.

When I work with a horse inside, I always put something on their feet to help them with their footing, either by wrapping their feet or by putting rubber boots over their hooves. I had a set of rubber boots that I really liked and had used in the past with great success, so we put them on my horse.

Before we started, I took my time warming up with my horse. I got him to walk, trot, and canter, and made sure he felt confident in his footing and the environment. Every step of the way, things went off without a hitch. After we were done, I inspected my horse's feet and everything looked fine.

We were all set for a successful afternoon. Then everything went to pieces.

I'd been using these boots for a while and they seemed to be have plenty of useful life left in them. They certainly seemed that way in the hour or so we spent warming up. From the outside, they looked perfect. On the inside, however, the rubber had started to breakdown.

A few minutes into the program, at least one of the boots gave way. One minute I was riding around the exhibit hall, talking to the audience, and the next the horse and I were on the floor. Or more precisely, I was on the floor and the horse was on top of my leg.

Both of us were shocked but seemed unhurt. More surprised and, if I am honest, embarrassed than anything.

My horse got up quick and was fine. I sat up, caught my breath, and then assured the audience that I was just fine. My leg ached a bit, but I'd fallen many times in the past and had been able to walk it off. My plan was to get up, check my horse's feet, fix whatever had gone wrong, and then get back on with the program.

As I tried to stand, however, I collapsed in pain. I could not put any weight in my left leg. I lay on the floor, realizing I was done for the day. And maybe for much longer. It turns out that leg was broken in a number of places. And I was in trouble.

All the work I do relies on my physical skills in the horse pen. You can't train a horse from the sidelines or sitting in a chair. You have to be up on your feet or in the saddle. And you can't be in either place with a busted leg.

As I mentioned, I had great friends in Jackson. They are dear people and immediately sprang into action. They called for an ambulance, which took me to a local medical center. They helped my crew as they checked on the horses and began packing up our equipment and getting them settled, so I didn't have to be worried about my crew or my horses. I knew they were in good hands.

At the hospital, I got bad news. I needed major surgery to put my leg back together. The doctor gave me a choice. I could have the surgery right away. Or they could stabilize my leg in a cast or brace for the long ride back to Oklahoma where I could be treated by my own doctor.

I was tempted to go back home, but I knew better. If I wanted to get back in the saddle my leg needed to be fixed right away so the healing could begin. Nothing good would come from a delay, even of a few days. So, I decided to stay and have the surgery, which was the right choice. It turns out that one of the best orthopedic surgeons in the state lives in Jackson and he was available.

This doctor didn't sugarcoat things. He told me my leg was in bad shape, with crushed bone and lots of fragments. It was likely I'd have some long-term side effects. But he was going to do his best.

He did better than that. With the help of more than a dozen pins and plates, he put my leg back together. It went so well that I think even he was surprised.

Now there are some side effects. I can't run as fast or as far as I used to. And there are some aches and pains. But still, those aches and pains are pretty minor. And, if I tell the staff ahead of time, I can get a security checkpoint at the airport without too many hassles.

Still, after surgery, I faced a long road to recovery. I was going to be out of commission for months. My leg needed time to heal. And I'd need pretty intensive physical therapy to get back on my feet. It was a long and painful process.

One of the exercises I had to do was particularly difficult. My therapist had me put the front of my foot on a block, with my heal on the ground. Then I had to lift the weight of my whole body on that injured leg. I like to joke that before the injury, it would have been hard for me to do that with both feet. Now I had to do it with one. It was excruciating. But I had to do it if I wanted to get back to work.

My therapy was guided by a simple set of principles. Do what you can, the best that you can, for as long as you can. I could not go right from my hospital bed to the saddle. But I could learn how to stand, and then walk, and then eventually run. And then eventually I'd find myself on the back of a horse. But that took a lot of pain.

Still, you don't want to give your future away because of the pain of the present. And with the help of great therapist and the encouragement of friends and family, I made my way back.

A few months after the surgery, however, I was at a crossroads. I had learned how to get around pretty well with a set of crutches and was making progress on my therapy. My doctor and therapist had cleared me for travel. But there was no way I could get back in the saddle or work with untrained horses. And it would be a long time till I was well enough to do that. That's when Charlie and his family stepped up. They believed in the work I was doing. So, they showed up and asked, "How can we help?" After some long conversations, they decided to come on the road with me.

Charlie was already an accomplishment horseman and trainer who'd been applying my methods for several years. We came up with a plan where I'd sit outside the round pen and talk with the audience while Charlie was in the round pen with the horse demonstrating the principles I was sharing.

To my great delight, it worked. At least for the most part.

On one occasion, I was so frustrated I got out of my chair and came into the arena to show Charlie what to do. I stood there with my crutches while he worked with the horse and finally got it right. The audience had a good laugh. And so did Charlie and I.

Still, it was not easy to accept that I needed help or to step out of the spotlight and let Charlie shine. I was doing all the talking, but he was doing all the work. Everyone's eyes were on him, not on me.

I'd been on the road for years and loved talking to crowds of people. It's mostly because of the message. I believe these leadership principles can change people's lives and make the world a better place. But there's also great pleasure in the work.

I've always loved working with horses. And there is nothing like encountering a new horse for the first time, especially a horse that's had some trouble, and helping it find its way. There's a moment of connection when a horse finally takes a risk and decides to trust me. It's their first step into a bigger world, where they can have a rewarding and satisfying relationship with their trainer. And the audience knows something important has happened.

There's a sense of wonder, when the audience holds its breath as the horse finally has that "aha moment" and turns toward me. You can hear it in the oohs and aaahs of the crowd when the horse begins to follow me around the pen, or when I ride a horse for the first time and everything I have been talking about—the power of relationships and trust, the important of winning someone's heart and their want-to—comes alive. I know that I have helped make that possible.

Now I know the message I am trying to convey is the important thing. I know that anyone who wants to can apply these principles, take the time to learn the skills we have been discussing, and can use them to build rewarding, trusting relationships. That's the whole point of doing these trainings.

Still, I also know I have developed a gift for this and I am good at it. The audience's reactions bring me a real sense of satisfaction. I've put decades of work into my craft and people trust me and listen to me because I have earned that right.

When I sat down and let Charlie and my team take the spotlight, I put my position as an expert and a leader at risk. People still listen to me, but I am not the center of attention. And they may begin to think that maybe I am not that special or important after all.

Remember what my friend, Lisa, says? Never take credit when things go well. I'd been preaching that for years. Now I had to put that into practice.

I could have said no to Charlie and waited until I was healed and able to return to the round pen. But that would have meant months of inactivity, lost income and, more importantly, lost opportunity. By letting someone else shine, the world could still go on. The message could get out, and Charlie and the rest of my team got the chance to earn valuable experience.

Now I did eventually return to the round pen, a little bit at a time. Charlie could still do the main presentations, but I was eventually strong enough to get into the saddle, with a little bit of improvisation. I'd climb on the fence and one of my horses would ride over and let me hop from the fence into the saddle. (It's kind of fun and a lot easier than climbing up from the ground.) Once in the saddle, I could ride around a bit and show a few techniques.

But even today, Charlie helps with my presentations. Sometimes he works with the horses while I talk. Sometimes he talks with the audience while he works with the horses. Having him do that reinforces the message that no one succeeds alone.

Had I not invested in Charlie, he would not have been ready when I needed him to help me out with Splash. And we would have all missed out.

Kami's story is different than Charlie's.

She came to work with me, along with several other students, as a college-aged intern and stayed on after her internship was done. Like everyone in an entry-level role, she did a lot of mundane work at first—feeding and grooming the horses, loading and unloading the trailer, selling books, and running errands. I let her start doing basic training with young horses and then gave her different horses to work with, so she could develop her skills. Then, as she did well with those tasks, I gave her more and more responsibility.

One early test came when I assigned her to pack up the trailer and get it ready to go on the road. It's not a simple task. We travel with thousands of dollars' worth of equipment—round pens, horse tack, ropes, training equipment, books, videos, and products for sale, and dozens of small items needed for my presentations.

She seemingly did a great job packing the trailer. Things went smoothly and the trailer was ready on time and set to go. But she forgot one step. Kami didn't double check to make sure she'd gotten everything. And as you can probably guess, a few things got left behind.

I have a rule for my staff: Lose something once, I pay for it; lose it twice, you pay for it. Kami knows that rule. And so, the next time she packed the trailer, she double-checked. Then she came asked me to check as well. She made a mistake and learned from it. Since then, she has kept learning and growing.

Like many people, Kami was not very comfortable speaking in front of a crowd. Since we're in front of the public in our work, I needed her to learn how to be comfortable with public speaking. But I couldn't just hand her a microphone and ask her to give a half an hour talk to a crowd. Instead, we started small.

During every event, we set up a small booth at the end of our trailer with books, videos, and other resources for sale. It's important to let people know what is available. So, I asked Kami to give a short promotion of one of our resources. I asked her to be short, sweet, and to the point.

I had two goals. The first was to get her comfortable in front of a crowd, which takes some getting used to. The second was to give her a small win, something she could build on for the future.

While she was hesitant at first, eventually she took to it. The more comfortable she got at giving short-promos, the more I asked her to do. She began to join me in the round pen and would demonstrate training techniques while I spoke and at times, demonstrate a technique or point on her own. All the while I would praise her, especially in front of a crowd. Eventually, she began to be a regular part of our presentations.

As we went along, she began to ask better questions about what we were doing and what she needed to do get better. She'd learned the art of self-improvement: making mistakes, taking halting first steps, testing new skills, and then gaining confidence as she learned what worked and what didn't. She's also proved helpful in unexpected ways.

I am an old cowboy and a long-time teacher. I'm comfortable sitting in the saddle or standing in front of a crowd and talking with them. Working with horses and with people comes easy. Working with technology, not so much. I like technology, but I'm not a natural at it. Especially these days, which are filled with constant change.

Kami, like many other people, is a natural at it. And recently, that's become more important.

As I'm writing this, the U.S. is in the midst of the COVID-19 pandemic. Tens of thousands of people have died, millions have been infected, and much of the nation's economy has shut down.

Big public gatherings—sporting events, concerts, conferences, even church services—have been canceled. And no one knows when they will start up again and return to normal. As you can guess, this has been a challenge for Leaders by HEART.

I make my living talking to large groups of people all over the country. That's the primary way I get this message out. But for months, I have been off the road and working from my ranch in Oklahoma.

The coronavirus has forced everyone to change. Things may never go back to the way they were. Even when the pandemic is over—and it might be by the time you read this—it's unlike we will go back to the way things used to be.

For me, this moment reminds me of the months I spent in physical therapy after breaking my leg. We do what we can, the best that we can, for as long as we can. I can't go on the road or speak to large groups in person right now due to the pandemic. But thankfully there are other options.

With the help of Kami and other team members, we took our operation online. We recorded a series of short videos called "Perspective 360: Looking at Life and Leadership from the High Road" and posted them on social media. And we began to look at new ways to connect with people, even when we can't be with them personally.

I could not do with this without my team, without folks like Kami, who know how to deal with this new technology and who are willing to trying to something brand new.

We don't know if it is going to work or what the future holds. But we do know that this current crisis has a great deal to teach us. Leadership—and in particular mentorship—rarely happens without challenges. There's no unbroken line to success. And just when you think you have something mastered—whether it's your business, your career, your organization—life will throw you a curve.

Many of us falter at that point. We love the success, but we don't know how to fail. We don't want to pay the price that comes with the constant pursuit of excellence. And sometimes, as this pandemic shows, the way forward often involves letting go of things we love or of things that worked for us in the past in order to embrace something new.

This is where a team can help us, if we let them. We can learn something new from someone else and let them teach us.

Sometimes we think of mentoring as a one-way street: I am the master and you are the young apprentice sitting at my feet, soaking up my wisdom. But mentoring is much more than that.

It's about a relationship, one where I invest in someone else and help them grow. Not because I want to get something out of them, but because I see something in them that is worth nurturing. It's saying, "I believe in you and want the best for you and, if you let me, I want to help you to succeed." It's saying, "You matter to me."

A good mentor also says, "Let's do something great together." We make space for other people to lead, so that we all can benefit. And if we are lucky, we'll build a network of deep, committed friendships we can rely on—people who we can trust with our lives.

I want to go back to a story I have told before about a horse named Spark. It's from my book, *Life Lessons from a Horse Whisperer*, and it's worth retelling here.

I talked about ponying two horses together, tying a rope from the saddle of my horse to the bridle of another horse, and letting my horse lead them. It's a kind of mentoring process, and something I teach my horses early on.

Often, the other horse is inexperienced, untrained, or aggressive in some manner and needs to learn how to interact with a trainer. So, my horse will lead them around and show them the way. It's leadership by example.

The horse being mentored is not often thrilled by this and will demonstrate their dissatisfaction in various ways. Eventually, however, they will follow the lead of the older, more experienced horse. The process is safe, as long as my horse keeps calm. But that's not easy.

No horse takes kindly to being bitten, kicked, or yanked around by another horse. Their natural inclination is to retaliate. But my horses trust me. They know I have asked them to do a job and they want to do that job well because of our relationship.

In this instance, I was giving a presentation with Spark, who was a well-loved horse that I traveled with for years, and I was riding him without a bridle. We knew each other so well that I could guide him with just a bit of pressure from my knees.

The other horse was young, high-spirited, and not thrilled about being part of my training demonstration. First, it tried to bite Spark. Then, it tried to kick him. Finally, the other horse bolted, which is about the worst thing it could have done.

We were in a rodeo arena, rather than in a round pen, with no fence to separate the audience from these two galloping horses. Since I had no bridle on Spark, I could not take the reins and bring him under control. Thankfully, he kept his head.

Spark turned back and looked at me for guidance. I prompted him to stop. He dug in his heels and began to slow the other horse. Eventually, the other horse responded, slowed his pace, and got under control. The rest of the training went off without a hitch, thanks in large part to the wisdom and maturity of Spark. He proved to be a good mentor to that horse and many others.

This never would have worked had we not invested countless hours in building trust together and pursuing excellence. Because we'd invested all that time, Spark had a well of confidence and power to draw on when he needed it.

It's the same for leaders. We need to develop deep wells of confidence, skill, and trust in order to pass what we know to the next generation.

At the end of our lives, most of us won't worry about how much money we have or how many titles we have collected. Instead, we'll worry about our legacy and who will carry on our life's work when we are gone. We'll ask, "Did I live my life in vain? Will my life have lasting meaning?"

That lasting meaning often can be found when we've passed our work on to younger leaders who can carry it forward. But it's a risky business. There are no guaranteed outcomes. Still, we have faith, and we decide to invest our time and energy in developing younger leaders.

We make investments without knowing the return or even without their being a return. Sometimes we will sow what we know into someone's life, and they won't get it. Or they will walk away. Or they will decide that the leadership path we offer them isn't right for them.

That's the risk we run. Still, we persist. We invest in our people and hope that what we pass on will benefit them in the future. And if we are lucky, we can help change the world. And set people free to change the world for the better, even long after we are gone.

Looking Back

In this chapter, we focused on the idea of shared success—that mentoring works best when everyone benefits. For this to happen, leaders have to share the spotlight and the responsibility for getting things done with those they lead. It's all built on trust, earned over years of working together, focusing on doing things the right way, and in pursuing excellence together.

Sometimes when you lead, you have to get out of the way and let someone else shine.

Some Questions to Consider

1) Think about a time when you had to let someone else lead? What were the challenges in doing that? What went well?
2) What keeps you from giving more leadership to those who work for you or who follow you? What are some ways you can make it easier for you to feel comfortable in doing that?
3) What keeps leaders from sharing success?
4) When was the first time you had to show leadership? Who opened the door and allowed you to do that? What did they do that gave you the confidence to lead?
5) When you hear the term "servant leadership," what comes to mind? Do you think of a humble leader or one that is passive?
6) What do you see as the risks of sharing leadership? What the rewards? In your own circumstances, which carries more weight: the risks or the reward?

Looking Ahead

In the next chapter, we'll talk about the end of the process and how those we mentor can become trusted friends and advisors. We'll discuss the need to let go and why a good mentor always keeps an eye on his friends.

CONCLUSION

Not long ago, I hopped in my truck and headed to Bowie, Texas, to see my friend Ben Baldus. Ben's a world champion rider and one of the most respected young trainers in the world. He and his wife, Cameron, are dear friends. Whenever I get a chance, I try to stop in and see them.

This time wasn't a social call. Or at least, not primarily a social call. I needed Ben's help.

When I arrived at Baldus Horsemanship, the ranch that Ben and Cameron run, they greeted me warmly. We sat and caught up for a while, drank some coffee and shared some great stories from the past. Then we got to work.

A bit of context here. I'm a good rider. I even won some championships when I was younger. But that was a long time ago. Since then, I've been focused on a lot of other things—leadership development, public speaking, coaching, and running my own ranch and horse training operation. I've not always had the time to improve my riding by practicing the fundamentals the way I'd like. Even someone like me, who has been riding their whole life, still needs practice.

Besides, to be honest, I'm older. At 60, with a leg filled with pins and screws and plates, I can't do the things I could do at 25 or 30. I have to constantly learn ways of working smarter and finding new techniques to help me improve or even just keep up. I try to do that while out on the road, meeting with horse trainers and other riders I respect. But recently I decided to take a few days off and dedicate time to my riding skills. Since Ben is one of the best riders and coaches I know, I went to see him.

He and I are also in the last stage of the mentorship process, where the mentor and the mentee become peers and friends. If all goes well, the student becomes the teacher. It's a crucial part of the process—one that takes intentionality, time, and often more than a bit of humility.

During our time together, I told Ben that now he had the chance to get back at me for all the hassles I put him through when I was his teacher. He got a pretty good kick out of that.

The relationship Ben and I share really brings to life the process we've been talking about over the past five chapters.

We first met in the early 2000s, when Ben was a 17-year-old high school student in Indiana. He came to one of our presentations and heard about the apprentice program I ran at the time in Pennsylvania. He had grown up riding horses and wanted to learn how to become a trainer.

Ben was also looking for direction in his life and thought our program might help him find that. He eventually spent two years in the program and then spent two more years traveling the country with me.

In those early days, Ben was a Tenderfoot, the first level of the Leaders by HEART training, which we detailed in chapter 2.

We'd go out on the road for months at a time, and, little by little, Ben learned the ropes. He learned how to care for horses, how to load and unload our truck, and how to pay attention to details. And I got to watch him as he learned and grew.

Along the way, he moved to the Broncobuster level, which we discussed in chapter 3. We focused on building the kind of trust and close relationship that makes mentoring possible.

In those long hours in the truck, Ben and I spent a lot of time talking. He's an early morning person and so am I. Our team would often be up at 4:00 in the morning, packing the truck and getting the horses settled in the trailer, so we could get on the road.

On one of our early trips, I asked him to load a box full of winter blankets for the horses on top of the truck before we set out. A few hours down the road, a thought occurred to him. "Did I strap down that box?" We stopped to check. He hadn't.

The box filled with blankets was gone, likely scattered somewhere on the highway, many miles behind us. Since it was going to be cold that night, we needed to replace the blankets. We stopped at a supply store along the way and bought about $500 of new blankets. We can't let the horses catch cold because of a simple mistake.

"Let's be careful and double check next time," I said as we loaded up the new blankets. He did.

Over the next few years, Ben became a trusted assistant and helper. He learned to pay attention at all times and be on the lookout for ways to lend a hand. Together, we went through the SERVE process that we described in chapter 4. Ben learned to focus on helping others.

While we were traveling, he talked about his interest in reining horses—a Western-style riding competition, where riders take their horses through a series of spins, turns, slides, stops, and other maneuvers. He hoped that someday he might make a career for himself in that field.

I tried to teach him all that I knew. After a while, it became clear that eventually Ben would leave and study under a trainer who specialized in reining. I told Ben about my friend Doug Milholland, the legendary trainer at the Waggoner Ranch in Texas, one of the largest and most prestigious ranches in the state. "If you want to work with reining horse," I told him, "Doug is the trainer you want to work with."

During his second year on the road me with, we were in Texas and stopped in to see Doug. As he is a friend and respected colleague, I was there to swap some training and riding tips with him. While we were there, I introduced Ben to Doug and spoke of his interest in reining horses.

"I'd love to come to work with you someday," Ben said. Doug nodded and said, "You can start tomorrow, if you want."

There was just one problem. Ben had committed to traveling with me until the end of the year, which was more than six months away. He knew I didn't have anyone who could replace him—not at a moment's notice—and that if he took the job, he'd leave me in the lurch.

At that moment, I was torn. I wanted Ben to follow his dreams, but he was also a key member of our team and would be difficult to replace on the fly. He'd become a Trail Boss, as we discussed in chapter 5, a trusted leader that I depended on.

Losing him would have been hard. Still, I trusted Ben to do what he thought was right.

"I'd love to," Ben told Doug, "but I have a commitment right now."

The next day, Ben helped load up the truck and went back out on the road with me to finish out the year. His loyalty and willingness to keep his word spoke volumes.

Over the next few months, Ben kept learning and growing. I also assigned him the task of training the next young apprentice who would take his place. When his time with me was done, Ben went back home to Indiana, kept working on his riding and training skills, and waited to see what would happen next.

It was not easy to let him go. I'd come to love and respect Ben and wished he could stay with me. If he had however, he'd never have reached his potential. We don't do the kind of work he wanted to do. He needed to learn things I could not teach him. So, I let him go with a warm hug and my blessings.

About a year later, Ben got another call from Doug. This time, Ben flew down to the ranch in Texas and took the job. He eventually spent six years at the ranch with Doug before starting his own horse training business, where he works with young horses and their riders, trying to help them reach their potential.

He's become a Foreman, as we discussed in chapter 6, a leader in his own right who is not afraid to ask for help, despite his great accomplishments.

Ben's also continued to compete, becoming one of the most well-respected young riders and trainers in the reining horse world. His horses seem to know exactly what he wants to them to do, almost before he makes the slightest to signal to them.

As he rides, he's listening to the horse. And the horse is listening to him. As a result, their spins, stops, and slides appear effortless. I wanted to know how he does it. That's why I got in the truck and went to see him.

When we went into Ben's barn and got ready to ride, he did something different. Before I started riding, he turned on a cellphone camera to record what I was doing. Then he talked me through a series of maneuvers, giving me advice as we went along. All the while, the camera was rolling. Then he got on his horse, and went through the same maneuvers, talking me through every step, again with the camera rolling. After that was done, we sat together and watched the videos.

All of a sudden, I could see my riding in a new light. I saw the difference between what he was doing and what I was doing, and, more importantly, I could see what he wanted me to do. Then we practiced some more.

I'd like to say that thing got immediately better. They didn't. I realized I had a long way to go. To be honest, it was a bit discouraging. The video showed my flaws as a rider. And Ben gently but firmly helped me get a clear view of where I was falling short and what I needed to do to improve.

In the video training, Ben wanted me to be able to visualize what I needed to do, so I can do the mental practice needed to improve my riding. He was also helping me work on muscle memory, so I know what to do and how it should feel when I was on the horse.

As we talked, Ben pointed out that athletes in other sports have been using video for years to improve their performance. Think of baseball players devouring hours of film trying to decipher what a pitcher might throw in a specific situation or what might cause a batter to strike out.

"We all have cellphones now," he told me, "so why not use the technology?"

Ben sent me home with copies of the videos and a lot of homework. That way I could keep working, even when I got back home. It's a training method I might have not thought of without Ben's help.

Now I do have a secret to tell about my trip to see Ben. When I want to see him, I was an undercover agent.

Yes, I went there to learn from him. But I also went to check on him. Even though Ben and I are peers and friends, I'm still his mentor. And I want to lay my eyes on him and make sure he's doing all right.

A good leader always keeps an eye on those they've mentored, no matter how much time has passed. Just because a person is far away or no longer works with us doesn't mean we quit caring.

That's what friends do. They watch out for each other.

I know about the stresses that come with the work he is doing—running his own business, competing at a high level, coaching other people, while trying to maintain a healthy life at home. I know the challenges that come with being out on the road and with experiencing fame and success—how easy it is to start believing your own press clippings or to get worn out and tired.

Plus, I had the privilege of performing the wedding ceremony when Ben and Cameron were married, and I want to make sure their relationship is healthy and strong. That's best done face-to-face, over coffee and meals, when you are not in a rush or distracted by phones and work or all the million things that compete for our attention.

Texting or a quick phone call just won't cut it. Those things are helpful, but friendship is built by spending time together. Being present with someone sends a message that they matter to you. That they are worth spending time with.

It also gives them a chance to stop for a minute, take a breather, and be themselves. With me, Ben can just be Ben—not the world championship rider, coach, or business—but himself. These days, when so many people spend so much time keeping up appearances and presenting an idealized image of themselves online, that's a rare thing. We all need time to be ourselves.

During that time together Ben and I had a chance to reconnect and talk about the things that matter most to us. He knew he could tell me anything. I'm probably the one person in the world he would come to regarding the deepest pains in his heart, because we have known each other so long and so well.

Since our last visit we've kept in touch. He called me recently and told me about having to part ways with someone who worked for him. The staff member had lied to him about something that could have put Ben and some of the riders he was coaching at risk. If his staff member had been honest, he and Ben could have taken care of the matter pretty easily. But he didn't, and so Ben could no longer trust him.

When you're in leadership, you look for honesty in the people who work for you. And you look for people who will care about the welfare of others. If someone on your team violates those two things, they have automatically chosen their own consequence. You don't have to fire them, but you have to help them own the full consequences of their actions. And you have to protect others from paying the price of somebody else's negligence. That is not easy. But it's part of the job of a leader and mentor.

In our time together at his ranch, Ben didn't just talk about the physical and mental side of riding. We also talked about the relational part of working with horses. And a lot about leadership. Successful training, he says, starts by having the right expectations. It's part of being what he calls a "balanced trainer."

"I am balanced," he told me, "when I am bringing the horse to his best potential, his fullest potential—when he is happy doing his job. The important part to me is the horse's confidence and keeping a happy horse."

Keeping a happy horse means having a realistic expectation of what that horse can do. When a horse owner brings a new, 2-year-old colt to start training, the trainer often has high hopes. They know their horse has talent and they dream that horse might one day win a futurity, a competition where a young horse competes against other horses their age. Winning a futurity can be a huge first step towards a successful career for a young horse.

"I wish all of them could win," Ben said. "But they can't."

To help come up with realistic expectations, Ben spends a lot of time with riders and owners beforehand, asking questions and creating a clear set of goals for the training process. He also works on getting a clear sense of what a horse or a rider is capable of.

For example, he'll ask a horse's owner what kind of shows they'd like to bring that colt to or what kinds of maneuvers they'd like the horse to master. Then he'll spend time with a rider and horse, seeing what they are capable of.

If a horse is capable of doing a 10-foot slide, then Ben will coach the horse with the goal of meeting that expectation and will feel good about being able to accomplish that task. If the horse can't meet that goal, then Ben will adjust his expectations.

It's a balance, he says—learning how to apply enough pressure to allow a horse to reach its potential while not overstressing the horse. Going too far too fast creates problems, he says. A horse will get scared and be worried if pushed too hard. "Then I have to go back, slow down, and rebuild their confidence," he says.

This applies to people as well. You can't push a rider to do something if they don't understand what is expected of them, or if they have a limitation that keeps them from reaching their goal.

There's a saying that helps guide our work as trainers and coaches: Never lower your standards; always adjust your expectations. The idea is to make sure that there's enough tension to prompt people to learn and grow without making them lose heart.

Ben took that approach with me. He pushed me hard but not too hard. And he always balanced his critique with words of encouragement.

I have to admit to being a bit down when I left after my first coaching session with Ben. I was sore, tired and not sure I could do what he needed me to do. But he believed in me and the video he sent gave me a chance to practice on my own, at my own pace and to put into practice what he'd told me. The next time we got together, things went better.

When I speak, I remind people that learning is a process, not a package. It's not a list of simple principles or techniques. It's a process of slow, steady improvement over the long haul. During my time with Ben, I've had the chance to put that advice into practice.

There's one last thing that Ben reminded me of during our time together. Find joy in the journey. Don't be so focused on a goal that you can't enjoy the learning process. Enjoy every moment on the way.

All too often, we see people who get so focused on a goal that all the joy has been drained from the experience. When the cheering is over, they feel empty. As Ben likes to say, winning a championship did not make him happy.

There was a great sense of pride in a job well done that comes with willing. But the real joy came in the journey to get there.

And now, we've reached the end of this journey.

I hope you'll be able to take what we've learned here and apply it to your own lives.

I hope that as a leader, you'll get a chance to meet people like Ben and Kami and watch them grow from fledgling newcomers to leaders in their own right.

I hope you'll have the joy of having deep and trusting relationships with friends and colleagues.

And I hope that when you reach the end of journey, you'll leave a whole host of young leaders who can follow in your wake, take up the torch, and pass the light on.

Happy trails!

Don't forget to check out:

**Leaders By Heart
Trailblazing Leadership**

35102 County St. 2740
Andarko, OK 73005

leadersbyheart.org

Also by Lew Sterrett:

Life Lessons from a Horse Whisperer

CPSIA information can be obtained
at www.ICGtesting.com
Printed in the USA
FSHW022341180321